PERGAMON INSTITUTE OF ENGLISH (OXFORD)

Materials for Language Practice

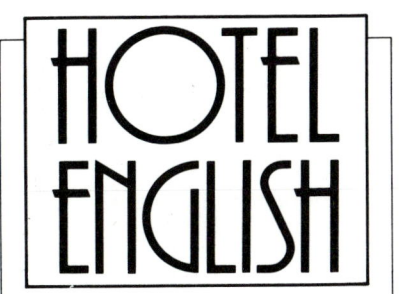

English as a Second Language

Helen Brennan Memorial Library

Other Titles in this Series Include:

BINHAM, Philip *et al*
*Restaurant English**
Communicating with the International Traveller

CRANE, Anthony
*Marketing English**

FITZPATRICK, Antony
*English for International Conferences**

McKELLEN, Joy and Mavis Spooner
*Business Matters**
A guide to commercial correspondence in English

ZINKIN, Taya
Write Right
A guide to effective communication in English

* Includes audio cassettes

English as a Second Language

Helen Brennan Memorial Library

Every effort has been made to trace and acknowledge ownership of copyright. The publisher will be glad to make suitable arrangements with any copyright holders with whom contact has not been possible.

HOTEL ENGLISH

COMMUNICATING WITH THE INTERNATIONAL TRAVELLER

Philip Binham, Riitta Lampola,
James Murray

PERGAMON PRESS

OXFORD · NEW YORK · TORONTO
SYDNEY · PARIS · FRANKFURT

U.K.	Pergamon Press Ltd., Headington Hill Hall, Oxford OX3 0BW, England
U.S.A.	Pergamon Press Inc., Maxwell House, Fairview Park, Elmsford, New York 10523, U.S.A.
CANADA	Pergamon Press Canada Ltd., Suite 104, 150 Consumers Road, Willowdale, Ontario M2J 1P9, Canada
AUSTRALIA	Pergamon Press (Aust.) Pty. Ltd., P.O. Box 544, Potts Point, N.S.W. 2011, Australia
FRANCE	Pergamon Press SARL, 24 rue des Ecoles, 75240 Paris, Cedex 05, France
FEDERAL REPUBLIC OF GERMANY	Pergamon Press GmbH, Hammerweg 6, D-6242 Kronberg-Taunus, Federal Republic of Germany

Copyright © 1982 Pergamon Press Ltd.

All Rights Reserved. No part of this publication may be reproduced, stored in a retrieval system or transmitted in any form or by any means: electronic, electrostatic, magnetic tape, mechanical, photocopying, recording or otherwise, without permission in writing from the publishers.

First Pergamon edition 1982
Reprinted (with corrections) 1983

British Library Cataloguing in Publication Data
Binham, Philip
Hotel English. - (Materials for language
practice)
1. English language - Text-books for foreigners
I. Title   II. Series
428.2'4'4647   PE1116.H/   80-42264
ISBN 0-08-025340-7

Printed in Great Britain by A. Wheaton & Co. Ltd., Exeter

CONTENTS

	Introduction	vii
1	**Choosing a Hotel**	
	Making reservations at a travel agency	1
	Hotel types	3
	Hotel facilities	5
	Press interview	11
2	**Have You a Room?**	13
	Room reservations	13
	Room types	17
	Room equipment	19
	Room rates	21
3	**Checking in**	24
	Registering at the hotel	24
	Hotel personnel	27
	Applying for a post	30
	Interview for a job	33
	Countries and nationalities	36
4	**You Are Standing Here**	39
	Giving directions within the hotel	39
	Giving information at the Front Desk	41
5	**Recreation Facilities**	45
	Some like it hot	45
	The nightclub	50
	Some like it cold	51
	Hiking	52
	Skiing	54

Contents

6	**Service with a Smile**		57
	Room services		57
	Other services		60
	Breakfast in the hotel room		63
7	**On the Phone**		67
	Telephone conversations		67
	Spelling on the phone		68
8	**How to Get There**		72
	Asking the way		72
	Travelling by sea		77
	Travelling by air		78
	Time on your hands		81
9	**Congress Facilities**		82
	Congress facilities offered by a hotel		82
	Types of meeting		89
	A conference questionnaire		92
	Arranging a conference on board ship		93
10	**Can I See the Manager?**		97
	Politely dealing with complaints		97
11	**Checking out**		103
	At the Cashier's Office		103
	Paying the bill		105
12	**Polite Phrases**		109
	Greeting		109
	Leaving		111
	Please and thank you		112
	Apologizing		113

INTRODUCTION

THIS material is designed for hotel personnel in work or training who deal with English-speaking guests of different nationalities and who already have a knowledge of English but need to familiarize themselves with the language and phraseology of the profession. More specifically it is for those who need to understand customers' questions and statements, to reply to them appropriately, to supply information from tabulated data and to produce statements and questions of their own.

The chapters are presented situationally and consist of authentic dialogues and information for reference and exploitation, offering maximum exposure to context rather than rigid sets of artificial language exercises. It is for this reason that the recorded material is so vital. Hotels and travel agencies in England and Finland have been chosen to provide a fairly flexible international setting.

Cassette One presents the principal dialogues and phrases of each chapter for listening and reproduction. These are marked in the book with the symbol ⊙⊙ . Space is not included on the tape for repetition.

Cassette Two consists of exercises which require manipulation of the items presented in the book and should be attempted once each chapter has been fully studied. The type of exercise varies according to the situation, having been chosen for usefulness or proximity to reality and not for structural features. In some cases guidelines are provided for correct production and in others the ability to interpret and respond to statements and questions covered in the chapter is tested. None of the exercises is self-correcting but a standard length of space is included in the recordings for the answers. Many of them are quite difficult and students will have to listen several times and make notes before attempting their replies.

The dialogues, phrases and exercises have been recorded at almost normal speed and with a variety of accents to accustom learners to the sort of language they have to encounter in their jobs.

The material can be used by students working on their own but is best utilised with a selective and resourceful teacher who can monitor performance and organize pair and group work.

Chapter 1
CHOOSING A HOTEL

Making reservations at a travel agency

The tourist season is in full swing. Here are two conversations in a travel agency.

Agent	Good morning sir. Can I help you?
Man	Ah yes, good morning. I'd like a hotel for a couple of nights.
Agent	Yes sir. What sort of hotel were you thinking of?
Man	Oh, something nice you know, and fairly central.
Agent	I think the Hotel *Angleterre* would suit you then.
Man	How far is that from the centre?
Agent	About half a mile from the railway station.
Man	And do they have a restaurant?
Agent	Oh yes, a very good one—quiet and stylish.
Man	That sounds the sort of place for me.
Agent	They also have a nightclub and a steak-house.
Man	How about a sauna?
Agent	Yes, they have four saunas in fact, and a swimming pool.
Man	Well, that sounds very pleasant. What sort of price?
Agent	Eighty Finnish marks for a single room with shower, 140 for a twin with shower, and 155 for a twin with bath.
Man	Oh, that sounds a bit expensive. Let's see, at eight marks to the pound that's close on £20.

Hotel English

Agent	I'm afraid that's the sort of price you'll have to pay if you want a really good hotel.
Man	What does the price include?
Agent	It includes bed and continental breakfast.
Man	I see. Well, would you book me a single room there for tomorrow and the next day please?
Agent	That's the two nights July the fourth and fifth. Just a moment please, I'll just check that they have a room vacant. Yes, that'll be all right. What name is it please?
Man	Darnley—Robert Darnley.
Agent	Very good sir. That will be 160 Finnish marks altogether.
Man	Do you take traveller's cheques?
Agent	Yes, of course. Please pay at the cash desk over there. And I hope you enjoy your stay.
Man	Thank you, I'm sure I shall.

Agent	Good afternoon madam. Can I help you?
Woman	Yes, my husband and I would like to stay somewhere outside Helsinki for a few days. Somewhere by the seaside if possible.
Agent	I see. What about somewhere in this part, by the Gulf of Bothnia? The beaches are really lovely.
Woman	What sort of hotels do they have?
Agent	Well, the *Grasshopper* hotels are very nice. This one, the *Sea* Hotel is about 250 kilometres from Helsinki.
Woman	How would we get there?
Agent	You don't have a car madam?
Woman	No, not on this holiday.
Agent	Well, you can either take a train—it takes about five hours, or you can fly, that's just a few minutes' flight.
Woman	What sort of amusements do they offer?
Agent	Well, in the evening they have a nightclub. Then they have saunas, a swimming pool—
Woman	What about the seaside?
Agent	There's a Holiday Centre right nearby, with a tennis court and various other games, and a very long beach.
Woman	Mm, that all sounds very nice, I must say. Look, I'll take this brochure if I may and show it to my husband, and

Choosing a Hotel

Agent	we'll come back and make a reservation tomorrow morning.
	Very good madam. We'll look forward to seeing you again. Goodbye.
Woman	Goodbye.

Hotel types

MOTOR HOTEL	A hotel with parking facilities and other services for motorists. Normally with a first class restaurant.
MOTEL	With parking and other services for motorists. Normally situated on a highway. With a restaurant or cooking facilities.
COMMERCIAL HOTEL	Normally situated in the town centre. Clientele mainly consist of travelling businessmen who stay for a couple of nights only.
RESORT HOTEL	Normally situated at a tourist resort e.g. by the sea or in the mountains. Clientele mainly consist of people on holiday who stay for a longer period than a couple of nights only.
AIRPORT HOTEL	Situated near an airport. Clientele mainly consist of airline staff and people travelling by air who only stay for one night.
CONGRESS HOTEL	A hotel with meeting and exhibition facilities, audio-visual equipment and banquet rooms for large and small groups.
HEALTH SPA	A hotel offering medical treatment, physical exercise and other recreational facilities.
SUMMER HOTEL	In operation only during the summer months. Often used as a student dormitory during winter time.
HOLIDAY VILLAGE	A number of small individual cottages or bungalows normally with cooking facilities.
HOSTEL	Modest, moderately priced, normally with sleeping and breakfast facilities only.

	Other types of moderately priced accommodation:
	  an inn (Br.)
	  a motor lodge
	  a youth hostel

Hotel English

Practice on hotel types

Exercise I You are working at a travel agency. What type of hotel would you recommend to the following persons?

1. *Mr Brown*: I'd like to do business in your town and try to sell this new washing-machine.
2. *Mrs Jones*: I'm flying from Helsinki to London in the evening and would like to continue to Washington D.C. early in the morning.
3. *Peter*: I've been hitchhiking from Munich to Frankfurt. Are there any cheap places where I could stay overnight?
4. *Miss Roberts*: I'm arranging the Annual Conference of British Hoteliers.
5. *Mr, Mrs Smith* and *3 children*: We are going by car to Rovaniemi and would like to stop somewhere for one night.
6. *Mrs Miller*: I have bad rheumatism and would like to get some treatment in pleasant surroundings.
7. *Mr* and *Mrs Elliot*: We'd like to spend a week's holiday at the seaside.

Exercise II Mention some examples in your neighbourhood of these different hotel types:

a motel
a resort hotel
a summer hotel
a congress hotel
a health spa
a hostel

Exercise III Interview each other in pairs:

Have you been working at a hotel?

Tell me what type of a hotel it was. (Sometimes a hotel can be a combination of several types.)

Choosing a Hotel

Hotel facilities

The Hotel Rooms

The bedrooms have a restful feeling of comfort with more than a hint of luxury. Of course, each room has its own private bathroom. The bedrooms are double-glazed for even temperatures and quiet undisturbed relaxation. Guests have independent control of the air-conditioning and a bedside console controls the colour television and radio and the room lighting.

There are penthouse suites comprising one or two bedrooms, bathrooms and living room. And there are two self-contained, beautifully styled, VIP suites. Each has two bedrooms and a double-sized living room. They are also ideal for use as private dining suites or for the small conference.

Wining and Dining

The Tower Hotel has three restaurants, all offering excellent fare and superb value for money. The Princes Room serves food and wines fit for a Prince and his Princess, and has its own cocktail lounge. The Carvery is a restaurant with a difference. Here, for a fixed price, guests carve for themselves as much as they want from succulent roast joints. The Coffee Shop completes the choice of restaurants, serving meals, snacks or just a quick refreshing cup of coffee throughout the day. The Thames Bar has its own terrace overlooking the ever-changing river scene.

Services

The Tower Hotel is ideally located for conferences up to 210 and banquets for up to 196. It is the place to choose when there is a need for a meeting place with charm and distinction, somewhere rather special, a rendezvous that makes the occasion a memorable event.

Hotel English

Practice on hotel facilities

Practise in pairs:

Exercise I
The Tower Hotel

1. What facilities are there in the hotel rooms?
2. What are the VIP suites like?
3. How many restaurants are there? (Mention their names also.)
4. What is the Princes Room like?
5. Could you tell me something about the Carvery?
6. Is the Coffee Shop just the place for a quick cup of coffee?
7. Are there any conference facilities?

GROSVENOR HOUSE HOTEL

Park Lane, London W1A 3AA. Tel: 01-499 6363
Telex: 24871. Cables: Grovhows, London W1

Grosvenor House is an international hotel enjoying both the atmosphere of Hyde Park and proximity to London's shops and centres of business and commerce. 'La Fontaine' is the à la carte restaurant with a view of Hyde Park. Its French cuisine is matched with a distinguished cellar.
'La Piazza' Coffee Shop is an intimate restaurant in the heart of the hotel. It serves international dishes, and is open for a quick snack or full meal.
Famous London designers have redecorated all the suites and bedrooms. The hotel's conference and banqueting complex offers unique facilities for international conferences and outstanding social functions. The hotel has its own swimming-pool, sauna bath and gymnasium, flower shop, medical suite, barber, hairdressing and beauty salon (run by Steiners), men's and women's boutiques, and theatre agency.

Exercise II
Grosvenor House Hotel

Practise in pairs:

1. Where is the *Grosvenor House* Hotel situated?
2. Could you tell me something about your restaurant facilities?
3. What are the guest rooms like?
4. What facilities are there to arrange a conference at the hotel?
5. Are there any recreational facilities?
6. Do you book theatre tickets for your guests?
7. Are there any other facilities?

HOTEL NEPTUNE

Location: 5 km from the nearest town on the shore of a beautiful lake.

Transportation: Airport 80 km, railway station 4 km.

Number of rooms: 233

3 suites, bath, balcony (2 suites with sauna)	23 single rooms, shower
4 smaller suites, bath	107 double rooms, bath
2 single rooms, bath	78 studio rooms, bath
	16 studio rooms

Number of beds: 441
Number of floors: 7
Elevators: 4
Check-out time: 2 p.m.
Laundry and valet service: 10 a.m. to 3 p.m.
Room service: 8 a.m. to 11 p.m.

Dining and Entertainment:
Fully licensed restaurant with Chaine des Rotisseurs cuisine and Finnish and international delicacies. Dancing, floor shows. Bar, Nightclub, roulette.

Special Features:
Several saunas, swimming pool, barber, hairdresser, massage. Car hire. Tennis, golf, riding, fishing, cross country skiing, boats for hire, sightseeing, illuminated footpaths, slalom slope and ski-lift. Lake cruises, National Park, observation tower.

Facilities:

Main restaurant	for 350
Congress hall	150—200
Private rooms (9)	370
Nightclub	200
Group-work rooms (13)	8—15
Bar	50

Exercise III
Hotel Neptune

Practise in pairs:

1. Where is the hotel situated?
2. How can you get there?
3. What kinds of rooms are there?
4. How long can you keep your room on the departure day?
5. When can you get room service?
6. What kinds of facilities are there?
7. What kind of restaurant have you got?
8. Are there any other special services?
9. Is there any opportunity for outdoor activities?
10. We are very keen on skiing. What can you offer us?

Hotel English

> ## Hotel Anglia
> Tel. 978-3411
> telex 9184 angfinn sf
>
> Distances: Helsinki 225 km, Tampere 138 km, Turku 160 km, Vaasa 195 km.
>
> 222 beds   110 double rooms   3 suites   salon for 500
>
> Nightclub for 210   Lobby bar for 70
> Banquet facilities for 800   Terrace restaurant for 240
>
> Various conference facilities for 10—250. Conference equipment.
>
> Leisure:
> 4 saunas, swimming pool, illuminated jogging track, sign-posted jogging paths.
>
> Holiday Centre:
> 40 cabins, service building, caravan site, camping ground, parking for 200 cars. Tennis court, curling pitch, volley ball court, skating rink, boats, children's playground, 5 km swimming beach.

Exercise IV
Hotel Anglia

Practise in pairs:

1. Where is the hotel situated?
2. How many rooms are there?
3. What kind of restaurant facilities are there?
4. What kind of meeting facilities are there?
5. What kind of leisure-time activities can the hotel offer?
6. What is the holiday centre like?
7. What kind of outdoor activities are there?
8. Is there a nightclub and what is it like?
9. Where can I park my car?
10. What is the telephone number of the hotel?

Choosing a Hotel

HOTEL SCANDINAVIA

Location: 70 km from nearest city

How to get there: airport 80 km
bus to the city from the hotel

Rooms: 42
2 suites, with bath and toilet
12 double rooms, with bath and toilet
10 studio rooms, with shower and toilet
18 single rooms, with bath and toilet

Accomodation for 64 guests.
Extra beds if needed
3 floors
2 lifts
Rooms to be vacated by 3 p.m.

Room service: 11 a.m. to 0.30 a.m.

Restaurant and other facilities:
Restaurant for 250 guests
Private rooms for 100 guests
Bar for 70 guests
Cafeteria for 80 guests
TV lounge, sauna, swimming pool, ski-lift, lighted walks, play-room for children.

The hotel is fully licensed, with dancing nightly.

The restaurant has a fine view over the lake.

Exercise V
Hotel Scandanavia

Practise in pairs:
1. Where is Hotel *Scandinavia* situated?
2. How can you get there?
3. What kind of rooms are there?
4. When do we have to vacate our rooms by?
5. I'd like to arrange a party for 100 persons. What facilities are there?
6. What kind of lounges do you have for hotel residents?
7. What kind of evening entertainment do you have?
8. What kind of outdoor activities can you offer?

Hotel English

Hotel Nordia

🛏		2 single, 32 double, 2 suites	
🛁 🧺 ☎		📺	Can be rented
🍽	for 300	💃	Nightly, afternoon dance on Sundays
🍸	for 50	🍺	Pub for 57. Tel: 3751
🌿	Sauna	🔨	Conference rooms for 100, 50, 40 (10 + 30)
CREDIT CARD		✈	10 km
SPECIAL		Car hire, guide service, ski rental	

Exercise VI
Hotel Nordia

Practise in pairs:
1 What conference facilities do you have?
2 Is there a sauna?
3 How far is the hotel from the airport?
4 Do the rooms have television?
5 Is there any dancing?
6 How many double rooms do you have?
7 Is it possible to hire skis?
8 Could you arrange a dinner for 150?
9 How large is the cocktail bar?
10 Can I pay by credit card?

Choosing a Hotel

Press interview

The Manager of the Hotel *Neptune* is being interviewed by a reporter from the travel supplement of the *Sunday Times*.

Reporter   How big is your hotel, Mr Lehti?
Manager   We have 233 rooms, with a total of 441 beds.
Reporter   And what about other facilities?
Manager   The chief ones are the main restaurant, for 350, and the Congress Hall, for up to 200 participants.
Reporter   What sort of location does your hotel have?
Manager   The hotel overlooks a fine lake, and it's set in a large park. It's very quiet and pleasant.
Reporter   And what do you offer to interest the foreign visitor especially?
Manager   First of all, the natural surroundings. Secondly, first-class service. And thirdly, a number of special features like riding, skiing and boating.
Reporter   Not to mention the famous Finnish sauna.
Manager   Yes, as a matter of fact we have several very good saunas.
Reporter   Do you have very much going on in the evenings?
Manager   Yes indeed. We offer dancing, floor shows, a nightclub and roulette.
Reporter   I see. Well, I think that's all for the moment. And we shall certainly mention your hotel in our next article on Finland.
Manager   I'm very pleased to hear that, and you can be sure we'll make our British guests very welcome.

Practice

Study this conversation carefully, especially what the Manager says. Then look at the brochure for Hotel *Anglia*. The reporter is going to ask you the same questions, and you answer as the Manager of the Hotel:

1. How big is your hotel?
2. And what about other facilities?
3. What sort of location does your hotel have?
4. And what do you offer to interest the foreign visitor especially?
5. And what about the famous Finnish sauna?
6. Do you have much going on in the evenings?

Hotel English

Useful phrases

Good morning sir. Can I help you?
What sort of hotel were you thinking of?
I think this one would suit you.
80 Finnish marks for a single room with shower.
140 / 155 for a twin with shower / bath
The price includes bed and continental breakfast.
I'll just check that they have a room vacant.
What name is it please?
That will be 160 Finnish marks altogether.
I hope you enjoy your stay.
The hotel { overlooks (the river) / faces (the sea) / has a fine view of (the park) / is beautifully situated.
What sort of price did you want to pay?

Chapter 2
HAVE YOU A ROOM?

Room reservations

Look at the *Lakeside* Hotel booking sheet on page 14, for the week starting Monday, 9th June. You will see that this hotel has single rooms with bath for 80 Finnmarks a night—these are numbers 101 to 105. The single rooms without bath, for 65 Finnmarks a night, are numbers 201 to 204. Then there are double rooms with bath at a price of 140 Finnmarks per night, and double rooms without bath at 115 Finnmarks per night. The double rooms are numbers 205 to 209, and 106 to 109.

Some of the rooms are already reserved. It's Saturday, 7th June, and the Reception Desk phone is ringing:

Reception Clerk   *Lakeside* Hotel, good afternoon.

Man   I'd like to book a double room for Wednesday next week.

Clerk   Very good sir, a double room for Wednesday, June the 11th. With bath or without?

Man   What's the price difference?

Clerk   A double room with bath is 140 Finnmarks per night, without bath 115.

Man   I think I'll take the one with bath then.

Clerk   That'll be room number 208 sir. And how long will you be staying?

Man   We'll be leaving Sunday morning.

Clerk   That will be—four nights sir. Thank you very much sir, and we look forward to seeing you next Wednesday.

Man   Good. That's all settled then? Goodbye.

Clerk   Goodbye sir.

Hotel English

The girl at Reception made a mistake. She forgot to ask what the gentleman's name was, so she could only mark "Reserved" on the booking sheet for Room 208 from Wednesday until Saturday. Mark this down on your sheet and take the part of the reception clerk for the next calls in the practice which follows. Don't forget all the necessary details and mark the sheet accordingly.

LAKESIDE HOTEL
Bookings
Prices: Single with bath Fmk 80 • Single without bath Fmk 65
Double with bath Fmk 140 • Double without bath Fmk 115

SINGLE ROOMS		Monday June 9	Tuesday June 10	Wednesday June 11	Thursday June 12	Friday June 13	Saturday June 14	Sunday June 15
WITH BATH	101	Marshall	Marshall					
	102			Johnson				
	103		de la Mare	de la Mare			de Freitas	de Freitas
	104						Solomon	Solomon
	105					Munroe	Munroe	Munroe
WITHOUT BATH	201							
	202						Dupont	Dupont
	203	Smith	Smith	Smith	Smith		Castle	Castle
	204							
DOUBLE ROOMS								
WITH BATH	205	Carpenter	Carpenter	Carpenter	Carpenter			
	206							
	207			Garcia	Garcia			
	208					Nieminen	Nieminen	Nieminen
	209							
WITHOUT BATH	106					Hemming	Hemming	
	107							
	108							
	109							

14

Have You a Room?

Practice

Woman　I want a single room next Tuesday.

Clerk

Woman　With a bath of course.

Clerk

Woman　The name is Jones—Jennifer Jones.

Clerk

Woman　Is that all clear then? I'll be staying for a couple of nights only by the way.

Clerk

You should have marked this against one of the vacant single rooms with bath for Tuesday 10 and Wednesday 11. Here is another:

Man　This is *Spearhead Trips*. How are things going?

Clerk

Man　We've got another plane-load coming in next Wednesday. Got any room?

Clerk

Man　Could you manage 4 doubles and 6 singles—for a week that would be.

Clerk

Man　Only 2 singles? Well, we'll have to put them up somewhere else. All right then, you give us the 4 doubles and 2 singles, and if we can't get anywhere else, you could put extra beds in so they could all get a night's sleep the first night, couldn't you?

Clerk

Man　By the way, there was a bit of a slip-up last time with

15

Hotel English

	you—don't know whose fault it was, but anyway—be a bit careful will you—it's me that gets the blame this end. All right?
Clerk	
Man	Got it marked down for *Spearhead* all right? Thanks a lot. Oh yes, we'll be coming in around 10.30 in the evening. We could have a drink afterwards if you've got time. All right?
Clerk	
Man	Cheerio, and keep smiling.

Well, your rooms are getting pretty filled up now, aren't they? Let's deal with one more customer though. It's Tuesday morning, June 10th, and a lady comes up to the desk where you are on duty.

Lady	Excuse me.
Clerk	
Lady	I'd like to have a room.
Clerk	
Lady	A single room for one night—tonight actually.
Clerk	
Lady	What price would that be?
Clerk	
Lady	Without bath then. I—I suppose you have some sort of washing facilities?
Clerk	
Lady	The name is Seaton—Mrs Charles Seaton—and—what time will the room be free?
Clerk	
Lady	I'd like to leave these bags somewhere.
Clerk	
Lady	Thank you very much.

Invent further bookings until the booking sheet is full.

Have You a Room?

Room types

SINGLE ROOM	A room occupied by one person.
DOUBLE ROOM	A room with one large bed for two persons.
TWIN ROOM	A room with two single beds for two persons.
STUDIO ROOM	A room with one bed and a convertible sofa. Can be used as a single or as a twin.
SUITE	A sitting room connected to one or more bedrooms.
JUNIOR SUITE	A large room with a partition separating the bedroom furnishings from the sitting area.
PARLOR	A sitting room not used as a bedroom (Sometimes called a salon).
DUPLEX	A two-story suite connected by a stairway.
HOSPITALITY ROOM/FUNCTION ROOM	A room used for entertaining (cocktail parties etc.).
EXHIBITION ROOM/DISPLAY ROOM	A room used for showing merchandise.
CONNECTING ROOMS	Two or more rooms with private, connecting doors. You can move from one room to another without going to the corridor.
ADJOINING ROOMS	Two or more rooms side by side with a connecting door between them.

Hotel English

Food plans

FULL AMERICAN PLAN (AP)	The rate includes three full meals and the room. Full board or full pension.
MODIFIED AMERICAN PLAN (MAP)	The rate includes breakfast, dinner and room.
DEMI PENSION	The rate includes breakfast and lunch or dinner and room. Half board.
EUROPEAN PLAN (EP)	No meals included in the room rate.
CONTINENTAL PLAN (CP)	The rate includes breakfast and room. "Bed and Breakfast."

Practice

Exercise I Explain what is meant by the following terms:

twin room   EP
junior suite   AP
display room   CP
MAP

Exercise II What type of customers would usually book:

a twin room?
a suite?
a function room?
an exhibition room?

Exercise III Book suitable rooms for the persons mentioned. Example:

Mr and Mrs Brown—I'd like to book a double room for Mr and Mrs Brown
for Mr Jones
for Miss Gray and Mrs Bridges
for Mr Jones, Mrs Jones and their nine-year-old son
for Mr Carson's cocktail party
for Mr Davies' product exhibition

Have You a Room?

Room equipment

1. venetian blind
2. curtains
3. desk
4. waste paper basket
5. coat hanger
6. reading lamp
7. bedside table
8. pillow case
9. sheet
10. radiator
11. easy chair
12. blanket
13. chair

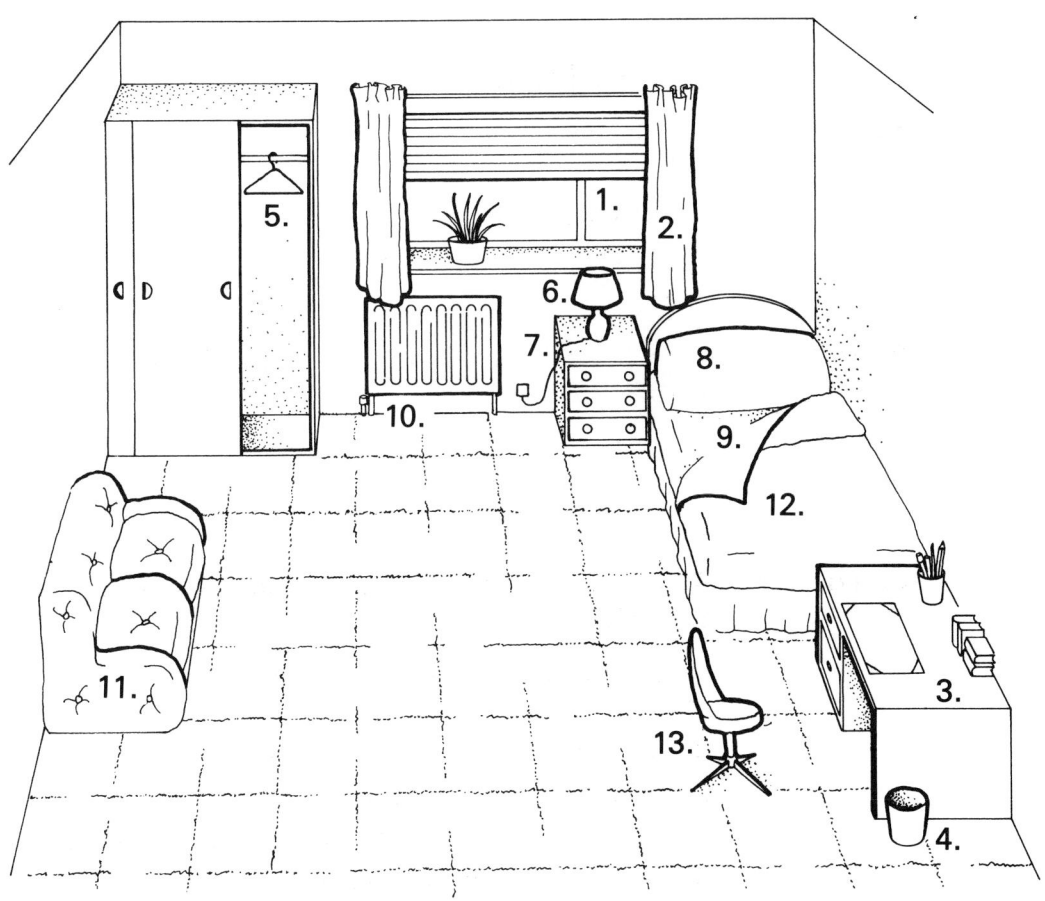

Hotel English

1. ash tray
2. telephone directories
3. letter
4. writing-paper
5. faucet (Am.)
   tap (Br.)
6. toilet
7. toilet paper
8. shower
9. towel
10. toilet flush
11. shower curtain

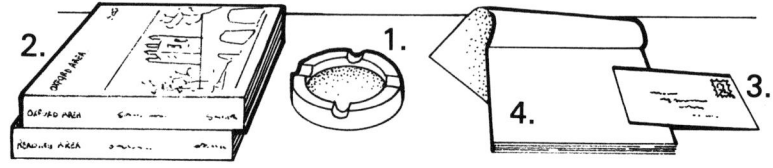

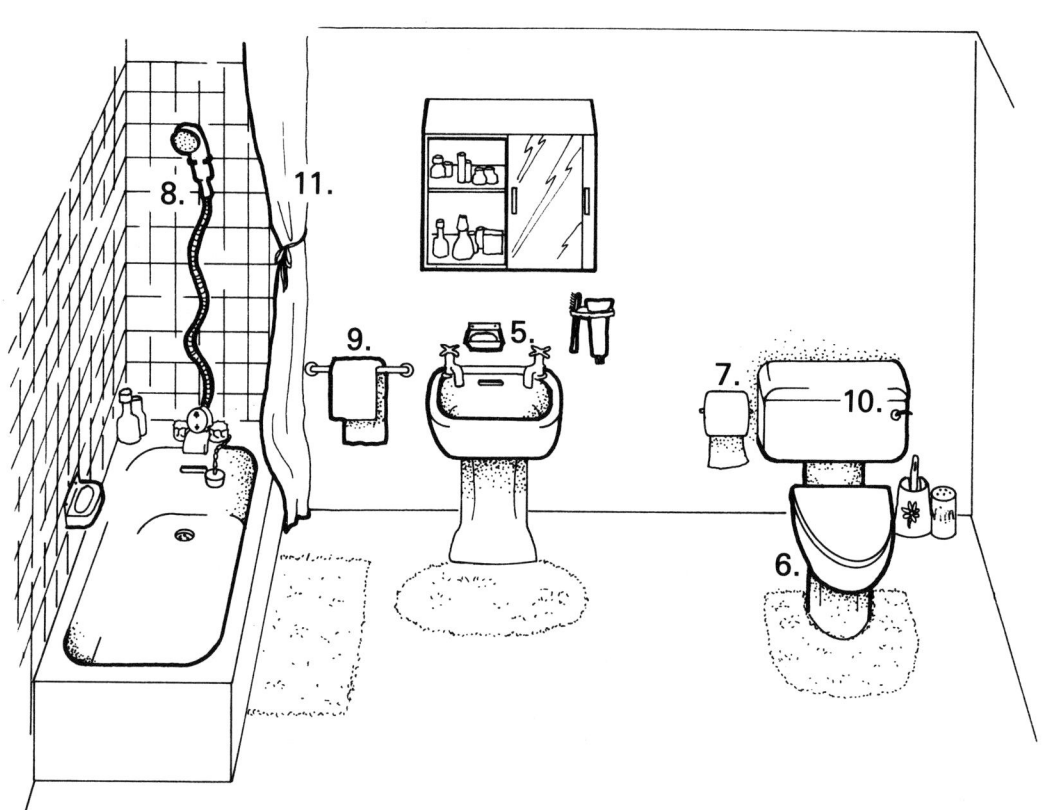

Room rates

HOTEL NEPTUNE

RATE LIST

Single rooms with shower	Fmk 80
Twin rooms with shower	Fmk 125
Double rooms with bath	Fmk 130
Studio rooms (1 pers.)	Fmk 75
(2 pers.)	Fmk 120
Suite with sitting room, bedroom, private bath and balcony	Fmk 300
Extra beds	Fmk 40 per day
Children under 12 years	50% reduction

Rates include breakfast.

All rates subject to variation.
Groups:
One night's deposit required 4 weeks prior to the date of arrival.
With a minimum group of 20 paying passengers, one person will be granted free accommodation.

Practice on Hotel Neptune

1. What does the price of a room include?
2. Is there a reduction for children?
3. What special terms are there for groups?
4. Is there a charge for extra beds?
5. Do you require a deposit to confirm a reservation?
6. Is there a discount for company bookings?
7. How much is the best room in the hotel?
8. What's the price difference between a double room and a twin room?

Hotel English

 # TARIFF

Queen's Hotel, Southsea
TELEPHONE - PORTSMOUTH (STD 0705) - 22466

ACCOMMODATION	ROOM CHARGE ONLY		
	1st & 2nd Floors	3rd Floor	4th Floor
SEA VIEW BEDROOMS			
Single	–	£4·50	£4·00
Single with Bath or Shower	£6·00	£5·75	£5·00
Single with Bath or Shower and Toilet	£6·50	£6·25	–
Twin or Double	£8·00	£7·50	£6·50
Twin or Double with Bath or Shower	£9·00	–	–
Twin or Double with Bath or Shower and Toilet	£9·75	£9·50	–
REAR VIEW BEDROOMS			
Single	–	£3·00	–
Single with Bath or Shower	£4·50	–	–
Single with Bath or Shower and Toilet	£5·00	–	–
Twin or Double	£6·25	£6·00	–
Twin or Double with Bath or Shower	–	–	–
Twin or Double with Bath or Shower and Toilet	£8·25	£8·00	–
PRIVATE SUITES			
One Single or one Double with Private Bath and Toilet, Sitting Room and Balcony	£20·50	–	–
One Twin and Double with Private Bath and Toilet, Sitting Room and Balcony	£27·50	–	–

Double or Twin Bedded Rooms let as Singles – Single Rate plus 90p
Private Suite let for Single Occupancy – £18·00

RESTAURANT - A LA CARTE AVAILABLE
Continental Breakfast 65p
Full English Breakfast (resident) 90p
Full English Breakfast (non-resident) £1·25
Lunch (3 Course) £1·75
Dinner (4 Course) £2·40
Afternoon Tea 65p
Room Service – per person 30p
Early Morning Tea – Single 20p – Double 30p

NO DOGS (unless arranged with Manager)

Please vacate room by 12 noon on day of departure

Practice on Queen's Hotel

In pairs, ask and answer the following questions based on the tariff list given. Answer with complete sentences.

1 How much do you charge for:
a twin room with bath?
a double room with shower?
a single room with sea view, bath and toilet?
the cheapest possible twin room?
the cheapest possible double room with bath and toilet?
2 When are the rates effective?
3 What are your private suites like and how much do they cost?
4 Can I have a twin as a single and how much do you charge for that?
5 Is breakfast included in the room rates?
6 Is room service included in the room rates?
7 How much do you charge for:
Continental breakfast?
English breakfast for hotel guests?
3-course lunch?
8 Can I take my dog with me to the room?

Useful phrases

How long will you be staying?
I'm afraid we are {fully booked.
                   {only have a double room available.
We have 233 rooms in all.
We are heavily booked for that week.
Service is not included in the room rate.
The rate includes three full meals.
We have a double room available with a rear view.
It has twin beds.
Are you with a company?

Chapter 3
CHECKING IN

Registering at the hotel

The Hotel *Mermaid* is a first-class motor hotel situated just outside Helsinki. It has 120 rooms, 70 of them doubles. The facilities offered include a restaurant, nightclub and casino, sauna and swimming pool. Congress facilities are also available.

Mr James Russell is arriving at the hotel. He goes to the Reception Desk, where he is greeted by the Reception Clerk.

James	Good morning.
Clerk	Good morning sir. Can I help you?
James	I've booked a room here.
Clerk	Yes sir. What name was it please?
James	Russell. James Russell.
Clerk	Thank you sir. That was a single room, wasn't it?
James	Yes, that's right.
Clerk	Would you fill in this registration form please?
James	I don't seem to have a—
Clerk	Here's a pen sir.
James	Ah yes, thank you. Now let me see—surname—Russell—Christian names—James Benjamin Francis—occupation—dentist—citizenship—what exactly do they want there?
Clerk	You put your nationality there sir.
James	Oh yes. British. Date and place of birth—19 July 1924 Cardiff—Address in home country—11, Shady Lane, Reading—Date and place of present entry into—Finland.

Checking In

	Well, actually I flew in this morning so it's today's date let me see—
Clerk	It's the 19th of June today sir.
James	19 June 1978. Passport number—when and where issued. Now where's that in my passort—ah yes—and signature. There. Anything else?
Clerk	Could you just fill in when and from where you have just arrived sir?
James	Shall I just put UK?
Clerk	Yes, that'll be fine.
James	Duration of stay. Well, actually I haven't quite made up my mind.
Clerk	You can leave that blank sir. And we'll fill in the rest—. Thank you sir. Now, if you'd like to go to your room. It's number 402. The porter here will take your luggage and show you the way. Here's your key—and I hope you will enjoy your stay at our hotel sir.
James	Thank you.

REGISTRATION FORM

Please use block letters
ANNOUNCEMENT OF ARRIVAL for police authorities

Surname	Where to? ....
First names	Date and place of birth..................
Address in native country	....
....	Citizenship ....
....	Passport No. ....
Date and place of arrival in country	Where and when issued ....
....	Duration of stay ....
Occupation...............................	Name and address of hotel................
Date of arrival at hotel.................	....
Where from?	....
Date of departure	Room No. ....
	Signature ....

Hotel English

Practice on the registration form

Practise in pairs a similar conversation between the Receptionist and a guest, using the registration form to help you.

Read the cards aloud when you have finished.

Practice

Fill in the missing words:

1 Please _____ at the reception desk over there.
2 Please_____this form.
3 Where was your passport _____ madam?
4 Do you have British_____?
5 _____ is my surname.
6 My first name is _____ .
7 What is your _____ in your home country?
8 When were you _____ ?
9 The _____ will take your _____ to your room.
10 Please_____the date of your arrival.

Checking In

Hotel personnel

Hotel Organization Chart

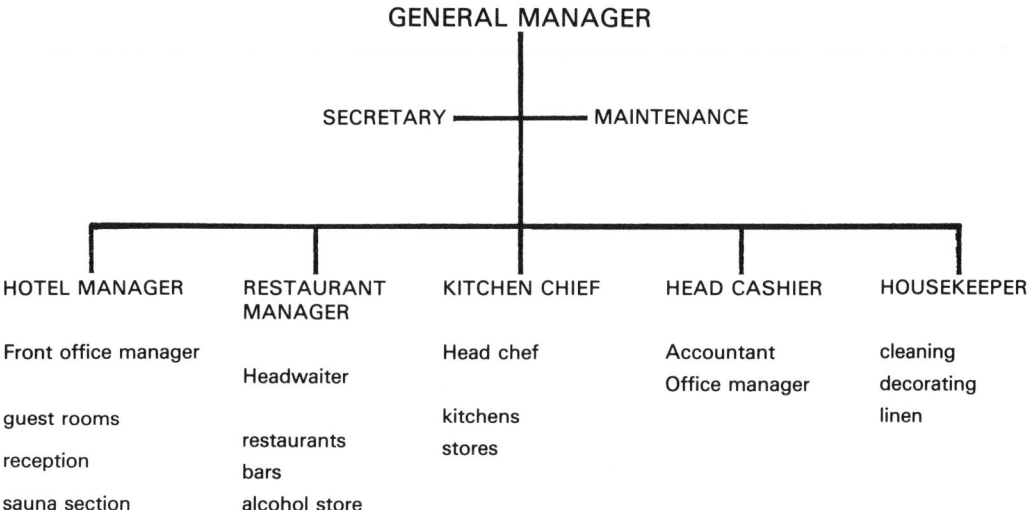

Hotel English

FRONT OFFICE MANAGER	is in charge of the reception area.
RECEPTION CLERK/ RECEPTIONIST	takes care of registration, in some hotels also receives room reservations and keeps them up to date.
ROOM CLERK/ KEY CLERK	hands out the keys and gives information to the guests about various hotel services.
CONCIERGE	arranges tickets for sight-seeing, theatre, cinemas and other events. Assists with table reservations and other hotel services.
FRONT OFFICE CASHIER	is responsible for the accounts and billing. Sometimes also exchanges foreign currency.
NIGHT CLERK/ NIGHT PORTER	takes care of the reception area during the night shift.
BELLBOY	shows customers to their rooms, delivers messages and mail and carries luggage.
PORTER	carries customers' luggage.
DOORMAN	receives guests, opens the door, orders taxi-cabs etc.
CLOAKROOM ATTENDANT	takes care of customers' coats, hats etc.
TELEPHONE SWITCHBOARD OPERATOR	connects the outgoing and incoming calls.
ELEVATOR OPERATOR/ LIFT BOY	is responsible for the elevators/lifts.
HOUSEKEEPER	is in charge of linen, decorations and general cleanliness of the hotel.
FLOOR ATTENDANT	is responsible for the cleanliness and often also room service of a special floor.
CHAMBERMAID/ ROOM MAID	cleans the guest rooms.
SAUNA ATTENDANT	is in charge of the sauna section.
STOREKEEPER	is in charge of the stores.
MAINTENANCE MAN	takes care of the technical equipment in a hotel.

Note: The above names for various positions may vary in different hotels.

Checking In

Practice on the organization chart

Exercise I   Explain the hotel organization chart.

What people work under the leadership of the General Manager?

What people are supervised by:

the hotel manager?
the restaurant manager?
the kitchen chief?
the housekeeper?
the head cashier?

Exercise II   Fill in the missing words.

1 _____ work during the night shift.
2 A _____ shows guests to their rooms.
3 A _____ counts the bills and changes currency.
4 _____ are responsible for registration.
5 _____ take care of keys.
6 A _____ carries suitcases and bags.
7 A _____ orders taxi-cabs.
8 _____ take care of flowers, linen etc.
9 _____ clean guest rooms.
10 A _____ is responsible for the guests' coats.

Exercise III   Practise in pairs asking and answering these questions:

Have you been working in a hotel?
In what position?
What were your duties?

Hotel English

Applying for a post

Here are some advertisements for hotel job vacancies:

Assistant Manager

The Inn on the Lake is a privately owned 80 Bedroomed Hotel with a considerable Banqueting and Conference trade.

The hotel maintains high standards throughout with special emphasis on restaurant and banqueting operations.

Due to promotion we now require an Assistant Manager with outstanding qualities.

The successful applicant will have a thorough background in all departments.

A high level of business acumen, flair in dealing with customers, and will be keen to take real responsibility.

Much job satisfaction can be achieved as the position offers considerable personal development.

A competitive salary and accommodation are offered.

Please write, enclosing career details to:
R. J. Roger, B.Sc., M.H.C.I.M.A., Manager
The Inn on the Lake
Shorne, Gravesend, Kent
Tel. Shorne (047 482) 3333

(375) A

Join the Ramada Management Team of
GENERAL MANAGERS
FOOD & BEVERAGE MANAGERS
DISTRICT MANAGERS (Multi Unit Responsibility)
FOOD & BEVERAGE SUPERVISORS (Multi Unit Responsibility)

Super-opportunities now exist for experienced management people to take charge of various operations throughout the country. We're offering excellent salary with definite advancement, bonus and incentive plans, top benefits, in-service management development programs and personal growth you'd expect from an industry leader. If you can handle success, tell us by sending your resume and salary history in confidence to:

Director of Management Recruiting
Ramada Inns Inc.
P.O. Box 590 JE
Phoenix, Arizona 85001

An Equal Opportunity Employer

We're building a reputation, not resting on one.

PENTA AIRLINE HOTELS

IBIZA PENTA CLUB
SAN ANTONIO / SPAIN

THE IBIZA PENTA CLUB is a 500 bedroom holiday complex, located on the beautiful island of Ibiza/Spain.

Our guests come mostly from European countries to spend their holiday with us, enjoying the three swimming-pools, selfservice restaurant, bars, discotheque, sport facilities, grill-restaurant, etc.

To assist the management in assuring the best of service, applications are requested for the following important functions.

The successful candidates should have experience in large hotels or holiday complexes in Spain or abroad and knowledge of the Spanish language.

— **FRONT OFFICE MANAGER**
— **FOOD & BEVERAGE MANAGER**
— **EXECUTIVE HOUSEKEEPER**
— **CHEF DE CUISINE**
— **RESTAURANT MANAGER**
— **BAR SUPERVISOR**
— **ENTERTAINER**

Applications — with c.v. and photograph to be sent to:

Mr A. H. Paulus, General Manager
Apartado 149, San Antonio
Ibiza, Spain

Telex: 68863. Phone: 340600

HOTEL MANAGERS
200-room luxury hotel southeast. Applicant must be capable of running a high quality food & beverage operation and be profit-oriented.
South Florida Golf resort. Applicant must be expert in golf course maintenance and have experience in resort marketing.
Motels 150 rooms. 3-5 years experience Applicant must be hard working and resourceful.
Send resume stating experience and salary requirements. Apply Box 6F, HOTEL & MOTEL MANAGEMENT, 845 Chicago, Ave., Evanston, Ill. 60202

EXECUTIVE HOUSEKEEPERS. Properties from 300-1000+ rooms. Current position must be at property with minimum of 300 rooms. Responsible for laundry, banquet facilities, public and outside areas. Hire, fire, train and schedule employees. Familiar with establishing and maintaining inventory control and security. FREEMAN STAFFING; PO Box F, Edmonds, Wash. 98020

Conference and Banqueting Manager

HAWKSTONE PARK HOTEL

The formulation of my management team, involves the appointment of a mature, professional to this key position, at this 50 bedroomed hotel and leisure complex, featuring extensive conference and function outlets and 2 fine 18 hole golf courses.

Formally, qualified applicants must possess a sound track record in line management, be a good administrator with the flair, personality and skills required to control future sales developent.

An excellent living in salary together with exciting career prospects will be offered.

Written applications with c.v. to: J. W. Freeman, FHCIMA, Managing Director, HAWKSTONE PARK HOTEL, WESTON, SHREWSBURY SY4 5UY.

(351) A

Checking In

This is a letter of application for the job of Assistant Manager at the *Inn on the Lake*:-

                                                                Hotel Arctic
                                                                Pohjoiskatu 12
                                                                94600 Kemi 60
Mr. R. Roger   FINLAND
Manager
The Inn on the Lake   28 March 1979
Shorne, Gravesend
Kent
England

Dear Sir

I am writing in reply to your advertisement concerning the post of Assistant Manager. I enclose my curriculum vitae, together with a recommendation from my present employer.

Yours faithfully

Seppo Laine

Seppo Laine

Enclosures: 2

Hotel English

CURRICULUM VITAE

Name	Seppo Laine
Date and place of birth	1 February 1956, Järvenpää
Marital status	Single
Nationality	Finnish
Education	Kouvola Comprehensive School 1963 - 1972
	Hotel and Restaurant School, Helsinki 1976 - 1977
Practical experience	Bus boy, Hotel Arctic 1973 - 1974
	Receptionist, Hotel Arctic 1975 - 1976
	Assistant Manager, Hotel Arctic 1976 - 1979
Qualifications	Able to handle the NCR machine Typing
Languages	Swedish (fluent), English (satisfactory) German (satisfactory)

Checking In

Interview for a job

Seppo Laine is being interviewed for the job of Assistant Manager at The *Inn on the Lake* by Mr Rogers. Here is part of the interview.

Rogers   Good morning Mr Laine. Please sit down.
Laine   Thank you.
Rogers   Now, I see from your curriculum vitae that you've only worked in Finland so far. Why do you want to come to England?
Seppo   Well, I feel I'd like to see something of the world, and get some international experience.
Rogers   I see. Now, our restaurant and banqueting is very important. What experience do you have in that line?
Seppo   The Hotel *Arctic* is known as one of the biggest and best restaurants in Kemi, so I've had quite a lot to do with that side of things.
Rogers   I'm glad to see you speak some German, as we have quite a few guests from Germany. Sind Sie in Deutschland gewesen?
Seppo   Ja, ich bin da zweimal gewesen.
Rogers   Gut, gut. That sounds all right. Now tell me, what would you say are the main things for an Assistant Manager of a hotel to keep in mind?
Seppo   I would say that attention to detail is very important. Making sure that every customer is treated politely and goes away satisfied. But also looking after the staff well, getting on well with them, seeing that they are happy too.
Rogers   Quite. And in our hotel we have staff from several different nationalities, which sometimes makes things a bit tricky. Now, is there anything you would like to ask about the job?
Seppo   What kind of accommodation do you offer?
Rogers   Ah yes. There's a small house about a mile from the hotel, or a large room actually on the premises. I expect, as you're not married I see. . .
Seppo   Yes, I think the room would be more suitable. Then there's the question of salary.
Rogers   Yes of course. Well, we are offering a starting salary of

Hotel English

	£3500 a year—plus meals and accommodation that is. But if we get on well we could reconsider that figure I think after a suitable period.
Seppo	I see.
Rogers	Well now, I expect you'd like to have a look round. Oh yes, one thing, when could you start?
Seppo	Any time after May the first this year.

Project work

Look at the job advertisement for the *Ibiza Penta Club,* choose whether you want to be an applicant or an employer and prepare for the interview. Applicants should prepare their letter and curriculum vitae and interviewers should prepare their questions.

Then act out each interview in turn using the appraisal sheets to assess the Candidates. While watching each group, also use the Interviewers' Appraisal Sheets to assess the interviewers. Compare and discuss your opinions afterwards.

CANDIDATES' APPRAISAL SHEET

Award points from 4—0. 4 = Excellent, 3 = Good, 2 = Fair, 1 = Poor, 0 = Hopeless

Name: _____ Points

1. Did the candidate seem confident or nervous? ☐
2. Was he polite or impolite? ☐
3. Did he give a good general impression? ☐
4. Did he appear to know his job? ☐
5. Did he ask sensible questions? ☐
   Total (out of 20): ☐

INTERVIEWERS' APPRAISAL SHEET

Points as above

Names: _____ Points

1. Did the interviewers take notes? ☐
2. Was the interview structured (logical)? ☐
3. Did the interviewers get what they wanted? ☐
4. Did they describe the hotel and the job? ☐
5. Did they give candidates a chance to ask questions? ☐
6. Was the general atmosphere of the interview pleasant? ☐
   Total (out of 24): ☐

Practice

Exercise I Interview each other:

1. When were you born?
2. What is your marital status?
3. What is your nationality?
4. What languages do you speak?
5. Where did you go to school?
6. Do you have any schooling in the hotel and restaurant field?
7. Where have you been working?

Exercise II Read the other job advertisements carefully on page 30 and list the qualities and experience that are needed for each.

Exercise III Write a letter of application for one of the jobs advertised.

Hotel English

Countries and nationalities

COUNTRY	CITIZEN	NATIONALITY	LANGUAGE	ADJECTIVE
Singular with the ending -*man*, -*woman*				
England	an Englishman	the English	English	English
Great Britain	a Briton	the British		British
Holland/ the Netherlands	a Dutchman	the Dutch	Dutch	Dutch
France	a Frenchman	the French	French	French
Plural with the ending -*s*				
Finland	a Finn	the Finns	Finnish	Finnish
Denmark	a Dane	the Danes	Danish	Danish
Poland	a Pole	the Poles	Polish	Polish
Spain	a Spaniard	the Spaniards	Spanish	Spanish
Sweden	a Swede	the Swedes	Swedish	Swedish
Nationality, language and adjective with the ending -*an*				
USA	an American	the Americans		American
Australia	an Australian	the Australians		Australian
Canada	a Canadian	the Canadians		Canadian
the Federal Republic of Germany (West Germany) / the German Democratic Republic (East Germany)	a German	the Germans	German	German
Italy	an Italian	the Italians	Italian	Italian
Norway	a Norwegian	the Norwegians	Norwegian	Norwegian
USSR	a Russian	the Russians	Russian	Russian/ Soviet
With the ending -*ese*				
China	a Chinese / a Chinaman	the Chinese	Chinese	Chinese
Japan	a Japanese	the Japanese	Japanese	Japanese
Vietnam	a Vietnamese	the Vietnamese	Vietnamese	Vietnamese
Greece	a Greek	the Greeks	Greek	Greek
Switzerland	a Swiss	the Swiss		Swiss

Checking In

Practice on countries and nationalities

Exercise I   Fill in the missing words.

Example: **Finns** live in **Finland** and speak **Finnish.**

_____ Sweden _____ Swedish.
_____ the Netherlands _____
_____ _____ Spanish.
_____ _____ Greek.
Germans _____ _____
Norwegians _____ _____
_____ Great Britain _____
_____ the USSR _____
_____ _____ Polish.

Exercise II   Fill in:

The capital of   The people speak

1 _____ is Vienna. _____ .
2 _____ is Oslo. _____ .
3 _____ is Stockholm. _____ .
4 _____ is Rome. _____ .
5 _____ is Moscow. _____ .
6 _____ is London. _____ .
7 _____ is Madrid. _____ .
8 _____ is Copenhagen. _____ .
9 _____ is Budapest. _____ .
10 _____ is Athens. _____ .
11 _____ is Paris. _____ .
12 _____ is The Hague. _____ .

Hotel English

Exercise III   Fill in the nationalities.

1   Pekka Lehtonen and Matti Virtanen from Helsinki are _____ .
2   Björn Borg is _____ .
3   Mr Bell is _____ _____ .
4   Monsieur Dupont is _____ _____ .
5   Don José from Madrid is _____ .
6   Hans Müller is _____ ____ _____ .
7   Knud from Copenhagen is _____ .
8   People who live in Switzerland are _____ .
9   People who live in Ireland are _____ .

Useful phrases

Would you please register at the registration counter

Would you please fill in this registration form

What's your occupation?

Do you have British nationality?

Where was your passport issued madam?

Would you put your signature here?

How long do you intend to stay?

And your Christian names?

When were you born?

And where were you born?

What's your occupation?

And your citizenship?

What's your address in your native country?

The porter will show you the way

Here's your key

The porter will take your bags

38

Chapter 4
YOU ARE STANDING HERE

Giving directions within the hotel

Here is a layout plan of the Hotel *Neptune* followed by some enquiries and answers about moving around in the hotel:

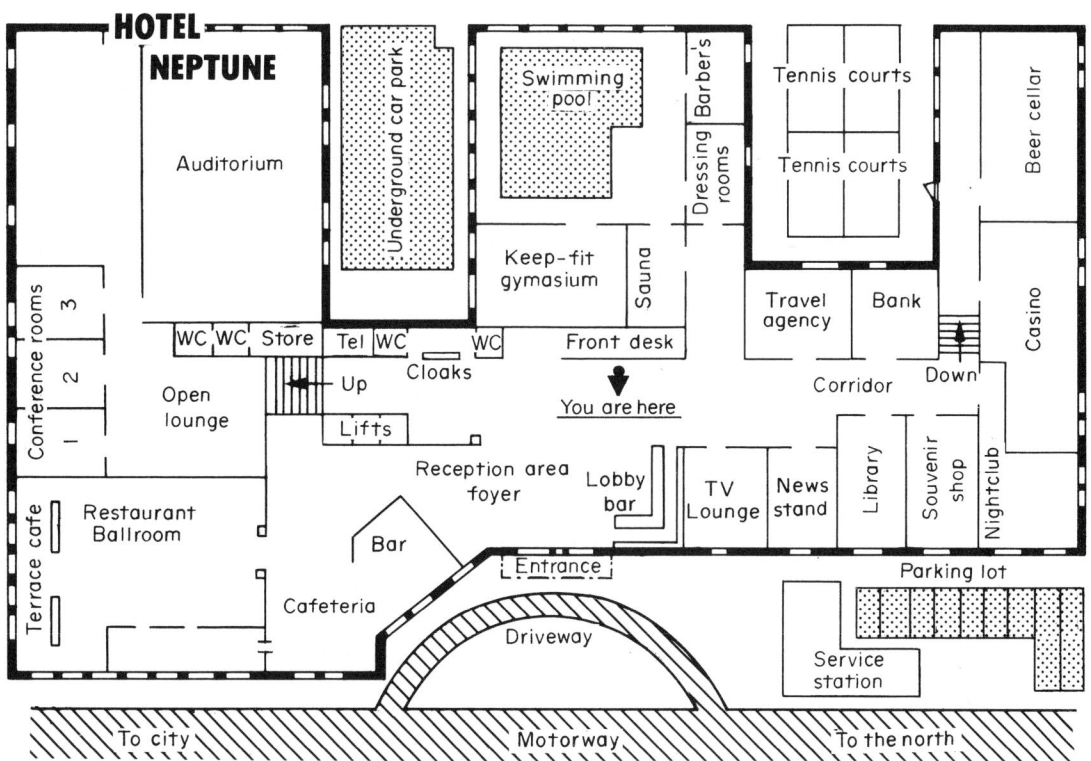

Hotel English

{ Can you tell me the way to the auditorium please?
{ The Hall Porter will show you the way.

{ Could you direct us to the beer cellar?
{ Yes, I'll show you the way myself.

{ We're looking for the TV lounge.
{ It's just over there behind you madam.

{ Where's the *Terrace* Café please?
{ Go straight through the cafeteria and restaurant and you'll find it just in front of you.

{ I wonder if you could tell me where the health club is?
{ We have a keep-fit gymnasium sir. It's round here to the left. Follow the sign marked 'sauna' and it's just next door to that.

{ Which way is the phone box please?
{ Along there to your left madam. It's just past the cloakroom and the ladies' room, opposite the lifts.

{ Is this the right way for the souvenir shop?
{ Yes it is. Along the corridor, past the newsstand and the library. It'll be open in a few minutes.

{ Is the lobby bar somewhere hereabouts?
{ It's right behind you sir, but I'm afraid they're not open till 11.

{ Am I going the right way for the tennis courts?
{ Along the corridor to your right. Turn left, go down the stairs, along a bit further and out into the yard.

{ I'm looking for conference room number 2.
{ They're all facing the open lounge. Along to your right, past the elevators and up the stairs.

You Are Standing Here

{ I seem to have lost my way. I was looking for a deer skin and they directed me to the beer cellar.

I'm sure it's the souvenir shop you want madam. I'll show you the way myself and you won't get lost. }

Giving information at the Front Desk

If you are on duty at the Front Desk you are expected to be a mine of information. Here are some examples of the questions that hotel guests ask.

{ Can I get a copy of the *New York Times* here?

The newsstand has a wide selection of foreign newspapers and magazines. }

{ What is the basic tariff for taxis here?

It's about 5 marks, but there is a surcharge after 11 at night and on Sundays. }

{ Can I get a car wash here?

If you leave the keys with the Hall Porter, he'll see to it. }

{ Can I get some hot sandwiches at this hour of night?

Yes—over there in the Steak Room. It closes at midnight. }

{ Do you have a TV here?

There is a colour TV in the TV lounge. Here is a programme schedule for this week. There's an American western or a BBC documentary. }

{ I'd like some tickets for Rigoletto tonight.

The travel agency in the hotel takes all kinds of bookings. }

Hotel English

{ I have to phone someone in Rovaniemi, but I don't remember the number. Can you help me?
Yes, of course. I'll get you the area telephone directory. }

{ When do the shops close around here?
Around 5 on most days, but there is late night shopping till 8 on Fridays. }

{ Do you have a lost and found? My handbag is missing—I must have left it somewhere. It's got my name inside.
Is it brown crocodile? The bellboy brought it in this morning. He found it in the lobby bar. }

{ Do you have any details about the floor show this evening?
Yes, over there on the bulletin board, you'll see a poster under the list of daily functions. }

Practice

Exercise 1 Fill in the gaps using one of the following. Each expression should only be used once:
ahead, along, behind you, follow the sign, in front of you, near, on the right hand side, on your left, opposite, past, right, right by, straight ahead, through, turn left, up the stairs.

1. The auditorium is over there _____
2. Go _____ and you'll find the bar right _____
3. Go _____ the cafeteria and _____
4. The keep fit gymnasium is _____ the dressing rooms.

You Are Standing Here

5 Go _____ the corridor _____ the travel agency.
6 Walk straight _____ and the conference room is _____ .
7 The phone box is _____ the elevators.
8 Go _____ and turn _____ and you'll find the TV there.
9 Go _____ and you'll find the night club _____ of the corridor.
10 _____ and you'll find the newsstand _____ to the souvenir shop.

Exercise II Look at the plan of Hotel *Neptune* and answer the following questions.
1 Where can I keep my car?
2 Where can I play tennis?
3 Are there any other facilities for sport at this hotel?
4 What kind of meeting facilities do you have?
5 What entertainment do you offer this evening?
6 I'd like to go on a sight-seeing tour, where can I get the tickets?
7 Can I buy some newspapers here?
8 Where can I change foreign currency?

Exercise III Fit appropriate questions to the following responses. Refer to the plan of the Hotel *Neptune*.
Example: It's behind you, next to the newsstand.
Question: Can you tell me where the TV lounge is?
1 It's just round the side of the Reception Desk.
2 Yes. Next to the service station.
3 Yes. Actually we have four.
4 The bank will be able to help you out I think.
5 Go straight down the corridor and turn left down the stairs.
6 Next to the sauna.
7 Over to your left.
8 Straight through the restaurant.
9 Around 5 o'clock.
10 I'll ask the bellboy for you.

Hotel English

Useful phrases

You'll find the phone box just *opposite* the lifts.

The TV lounge is over there *behind you.*

The cloakroom is *next to* the reception desk.

Turn (*to the*) *left* and you'll find the gymnasium on *the right hand side of* the corridor.

Pass the newsstand and *turn right.*

Go down the stairs and you'll find the beer cellar in the basement.

Go up the stairs.

Follow the sign and you'll find the auditorium on the first floor.

Carry straight on. You can't miss it.

I'm afraid you will have to go into town for (that).

Chapter 5
RECREATION FACILITIES

Some like it hot

Now we're going to learn more about the facilities that the Hotel *Neptune* has to offer.
Here is a conversation about keep-fit facilities between a hotel resident and the Reception Clerk.

Guest   My doctor has told me I must keep in good physical condition. I hear that your hotel is one of the best ones in the country for that kind of thing. Could you tell me what facilities you have here?

Clerk   Well, we have a well-equipped keep-fit gymnasium with all the latest recreational sports apparatus—exercise bicycle, weights, wall bars—that sort of thing.

Guest   That sounds very interesting.

Clerk   Then we have two excellent saunas including a smoke sauna. By the way there's a free supply of towels and Finnish sauna soap.

Guest   Very good and what about a swim?

Clerk   Yes, you can have a dip in our heated swimming pool which contains a special salt in the water to stimulate the skin. You can also borrow swimming trunks free of charge.

Guest   Oh good. I've left mine at home.

Clerk   And afterwards you can relax with beer or soft drinks

Hotel English

Guest   and sausages in the after-sauna room where there's a large open fireplace with birch logs.
Guest   How about outdoor activities?
Clerk   We have a nine-hole golf course or if you prefer you can water-ski on the lake or hire a rowing boat if you feel energetic.
Guest   Do you have any tennis courts?
Clerk   Oh yes and you can also play badminton. Racquets and balls are available at a small charge. And if that's not enough there is always croquet on the lawn.

Practice

Exercise I   Express the following in a different way using the word(s) in brackets:

1. Many keep-fit activities are possible in the hotel. (facilities)
2. The gymnasium is very modern. (well-equipped/sports apparatus)
3. We do not charge for the use of the towels and soap. (free supply)
4. Water skis and rowing boats are lent. (hire)
5. We also provide racquets and balls for tennis. (available)
6. They do not cost very much. (small charge)

Exercise II   Take the part of the hotel clerk and answer these enquiries:

1. What's so special about the swimming pool?
2. What sort of equipment is there in the gymnasium?
3. I'm feeling energetic. What do you suggest?
4. How do I go about using the sauna?

Recreation Facilities

Here is a conversation about the sauna

Jane   Yesterday we were invited by some Finns to have a bath with them.

Peter   That's a bit strange, isn't it?

Jane   Well, first we went into the changing room and took off all our clothes.

Peter   Yes.

Jane   And then put them on coathangers with our towels. Then we went into the washroom without a stitch on.

Peter   You mean stark naked?

Jane   Yes, and then we picked up a little wooden sauna pail and filled it with warm water and armed ourselves with two birch switches.

Peter   What are they for?

Jane   Well, they're made from soft birch twigs and you're supposed to dip them in the warm water and briskly whisk them over your skin.

Peter   That sounds nice. Do you get to beat other people as well?

Jane   Yes. Anyway we all troop into the sauna proper—which is the hot room. And it is hot—the heat knocked me back when I stepped in.

Peter   What temperature is it then?

Jane   About 100° (degrees) centigrade—higher on the higher levels.

Peter   Sounds like real torture. Where does the heat come from?

Jane   There's a stove in the sauna, fired with wood, and on top of the stove a pile of stones which keep the heat. Sometimes the stove works on electricity, but then the sauna is often too hot. Then the idea is to throw some water on the stones and "löyly" or dry steam is given off.

Peter   What does that do?

Jane   The effect is to step up the blood circulation and produce vigorous perspiration.

Peter   You mean you sweat. Sounds like the madman who was

Hotel English

	banging his head against the wall until someone came up and asked him why.
Jane	And what did he say?
Peter	"Its so nice when I stop."
Jane	Yes, sauna is a bit like that. After 10 minutes or so it's time to cool off under a shower or go for a quick swim. It's really marvellous to take a dip in the cool water of the lake and in winter they even cut a hole in the ice for you to plunge into.
Peter	Sounds crazy to me!
Jane	Actually it's great fun. We went back into the sauna three times.
Peter	You're certainly a glutton for punishment. What happens then?
Jane	Then it's time to wash yourself, or rather to be washed. A large washer-woman comes in to scrub every part of you.
Peter	Even your hair?
Jane	Yes. Finally it's time to wrap yourself up in your sauna robe and take a sauna snack—that usually consists of grilled sauna sausage and a glass of cool Finnish beer. You can't imagine what a wonderful feeling of relaxation you have—with your skin all glowing—you really feel content and at peace with the world. It's one of the great pleasures of life.
Peter	I'm sure it is, especially if you happen to be a Finn.

Practice

Exercise I   Fill in the gaps with suitable words or phrases

1 First go to the _____ and take your clothes _____ .
2 Then take a birch _____ and go to the sauna.
3 Throw some warm water on the stones of the _____ .
4 Relax in the heat until you start to_____ .
5 Then you can beat yourself with the birch _____ to make your blood _____ .
6 Cool _____ under a cold _____ or go for a quick swim.
7 Go to the _____ and wash yourself.

Exercise II   A foreigner comes up to you and asks:
What exactly is a "sauna"?
Tell him in your own words.

Hotel English

The nightclub

NIGHTCLUB OPEN 8 P.M. TILL 3 A.M.

Dancing every night   DISCO — all the latest pop records
Every evening — GAMBRINI at the piano in the Restaurant

Thursday evening is JAZZ evening
Friday evening is ROCK night
Saturday evening is GUEST STAR evening

Friday   THE NITWITS
— leading Finnish
rock, pop and folk band

Saturday   from Hollywood the fabulous
Miss STELLA CARR
(cover charge 30 Fmk)

CASINO with ROULETTE table OPEN from 9 p.m. to midnight
BEER CELLAR
TWICE NIGHTLY 'GERMAN DRINKING SONGS'

Practice

A guest telephones you at the hotel to ask about the nightclub. How would you describe its attractions?

Some like it cold

On the western peak of the 700 metres (2,200 ft) high Bear Mountain in the heart of fell Lapland stands Hotel *Karhu*, just below the treeline. Bear Mountain is of ancient geological origin, and the Ice Age has left its traces throughout the area. The grey-green granite of the district is becoming increasingly sought-after for decorative building purposes. For centuries Bear Mountain has been a holy place for the Lapps. Set in a National Park stretching north-eastwards for 50 miles, the Hotel *Karhu* is a modern recreation centre with all the facilities for outdoor activities. The hotel is located halfway up the mountain with a splendid panorama view. Excursions to Lapp villages and reindeer farms are regularly arranged. Outdoor activities include hiking, rowing and fishing during the long summer days. But it is for its winter sports that the Hotel is best known. Bear Mountain has the longest downhill ski slope in the country, and the numerous marked trails offer excellent cross-country skiing in exciting scenery in winter, and equally fine walks when the snow has melted away.

Practice

Express the following in a different way using the word(s) in brackets:

1 You can see the effect of the Ice Age everywhere. (traces/-left)
2 Many people like the granite for building with. (increasingly sought after)
3 A lot of outdoor recreation is possible at the Hotel *Karhu*. (facilities)
4 There is a good view from the hotel because it is on the mountainside. (located/halfway)
5 Most people go to the hotel for winter sports. (best known)

Hotel English

Hiking

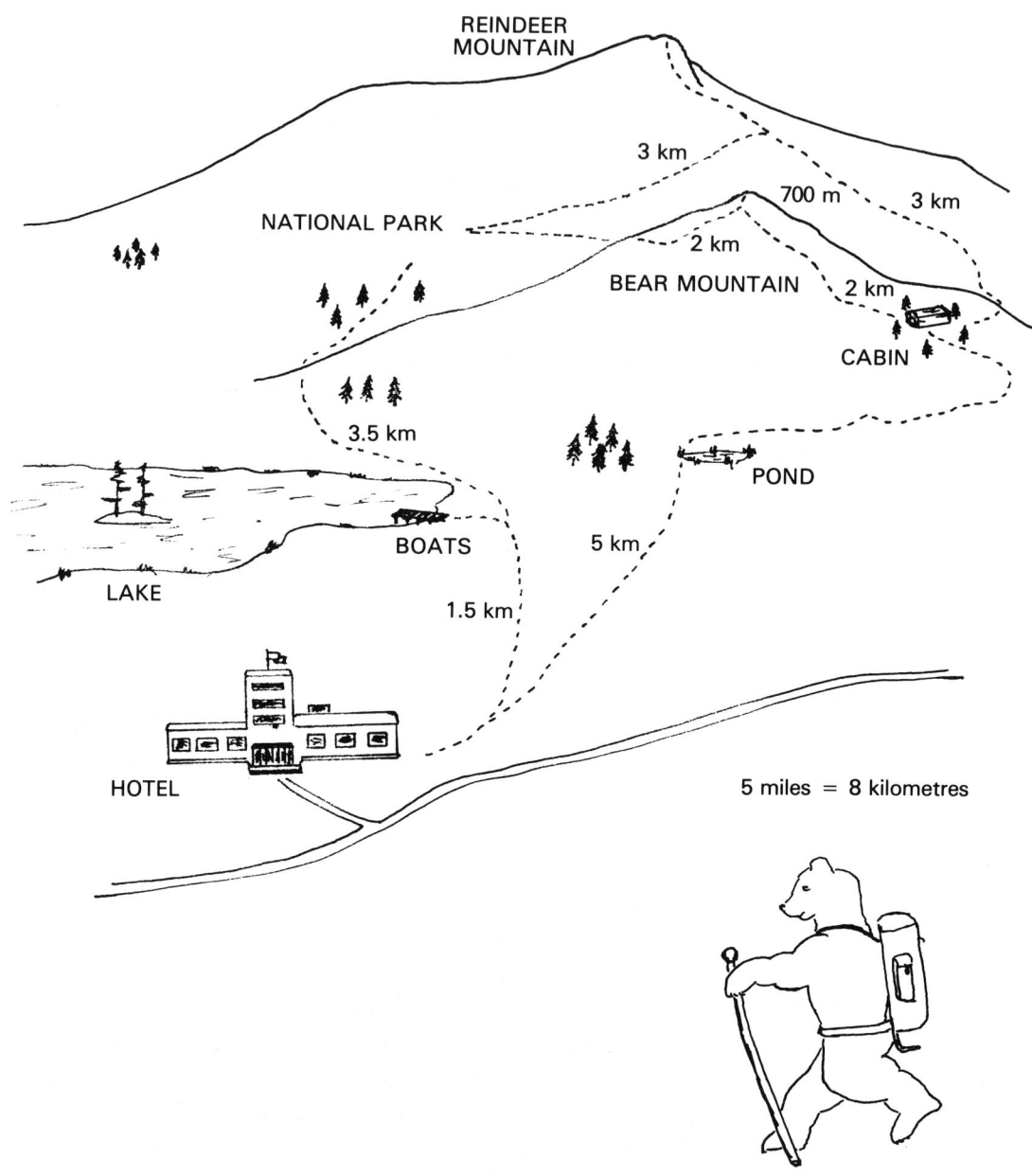

Recreation Facilities

Leila is at the Reception Desk of the Hotel *Karhu* in summertime. A number of guests come and ask her questions. She gives them advice with the help of the map.

1st guest   I'd like to take a boat out today. How do I get down to the lake?

Leila   Drive down to the main road and then turn left—it's about half a mile from the road junction.

1st guest   But couldn't I walk?

Leila   Oh yes. If you take the trail it's about half a mile. The trail is marked blue. And there will be a man there looking after the boats.

1st guest   I see. Thank you very much.

Leila   You're welcome.—Yes sir?

2nd guest   My wife and I would like a good long hike today. What would you recommend?

Leila   Well, if you haven't been walking here before, I'd suggest you go past Bear Pond and on to the cabin—you can make coffee there if you like. Then come back through the gully—it's very pretty and not too steep. You'll get to the top of the fell that way—the view should be wonderful on a clear day like this—then down the other side, and back to the hotel.

2nd guest   How far would that be?

Leila   Let me see—5 plus 2, that's 7, and 2, 9, and 3½, twelve and a half kilometres—nearly 8 miles.

2nd guest   That sounds fine. Thank you.

Leila   Thank you sir.

3rd guest   Excuse me...

Leila   Can I help you sir?

3rd guest   I'd like to do some fishing.

Leila   Do you have a licence?

3rd guest   No, as a matter of fact I don't.

Leila   Then would you please fill in this form? The charge is 20 marks for each day's fishing.

3rd guest   I see. Thank you. And where would I do best to go?

Leila   There are pike, perch and whitefish in the lake. Then there are trout in the pond, but I'm told the fishing hasn't been too good there lately.

3rd guest   I see. Perhaps I'd better try my luck down at the lake first.

Hotel English

Practice

Exercise 1   Now you are at the Reception Desk, and a number of guests come and ask you for advice. Using the map, help them as much as you can.

1   I'd like to go for a fairly short walk. Could you recommend one?
2   We'd like to go to Reindeer Fell. How far is it?
3   Can I do some fishing here?
4   I'd like to go through one of your famous canyons. Do you have one here?
5   Where can I get a boat?

Skiing

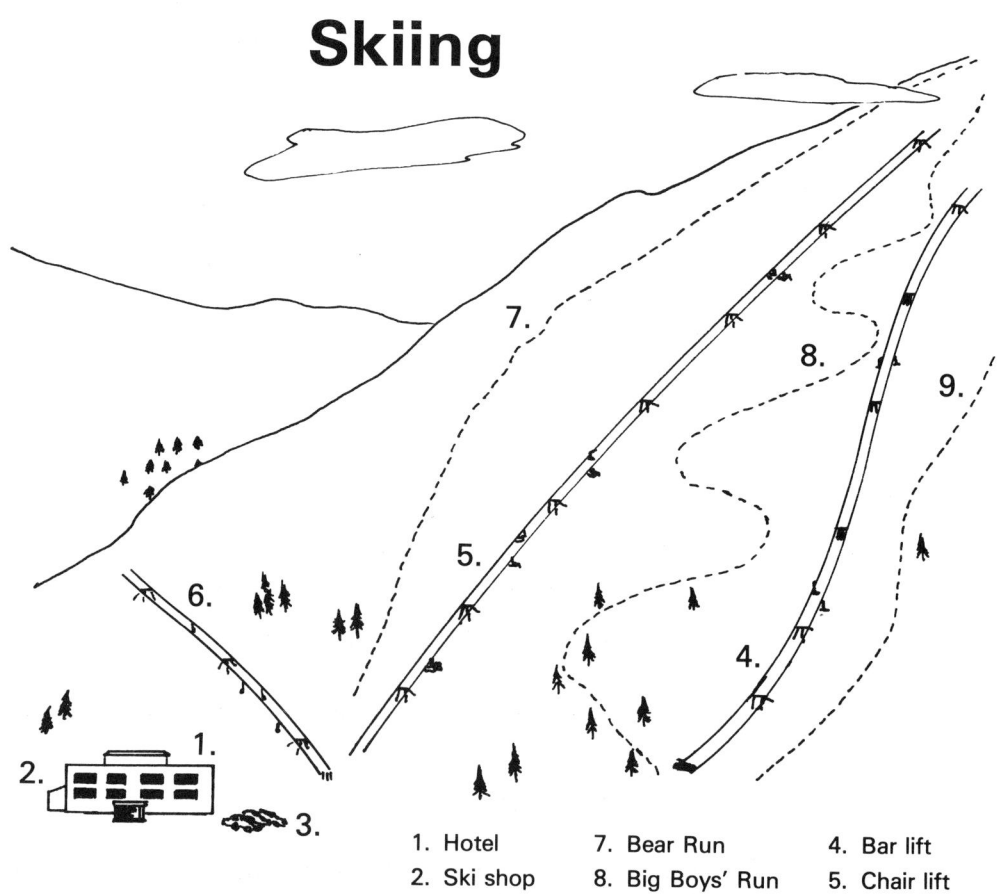

1. Hotel
2. Ski shop
3. Parking lot
7. Bear Run
8. Big Boys' Run
9. Sunshine Slope
4. Bar lift
5. Chair lift
6. Ski-school lift

Recreation Facilities

SKI WITH THE BEAR

Ski School
1 week course 140 Fmk per person
1 day course   50 Fmk per person
Private lesson   40 Fmk per hour

Rent-a-Ski (Prices per day)
Slalom skis   20 Fmk
Slalom boots   15 Fmk
Slalom ski sticks   5 Fmk
Cross-country skis   10 Fmk
Cross-country boots   8 Fmk
Cross-country ski sticks 5 Fmk

Ski Lifts
Bar lift   30 Fmk for 20 trips
Chair lift 40 Fmk for 20 trips
Ski-school lift 20 Fmk for 20 trips
One day   50 Fmk
One week 220 Fmk
Whole season 500 Fmk
For second family member 400 Fmk
For third family member   300 Fmk

Practice

Exercise I You are again at the Desk of the Hotel *Karhu*. A number of guests ask you questions about the downhill ski slopes and prices for renting equipment. Answer them as well as you can, using the information in the diagram and the *Ski with the bear* brochure.

1 How many lifts do you have and what kind are they?
2 Are the slopes far from the hotel?
3 Which is the sunniest slope would you say?
4 Do you have any easy runs?
5 Can I get instruction?
6 How much does instruction cost per day?
7 I need to rent downhill ski equipment. What will it cost me?
8 My ski-bindings have come loose. Can I get them fixed anywhere here?
9 What do the lifts cost here?

Exercise II Break up into pairs and ask each other questions about skiing at Hotel *Karhu*.

Hotel English

Useful phrases

A well-equipped keep-fit gymnasium...
... with all the latest apparatus
A free supply (of towels)
Free of charge
Available at a small charge
With a splendid view
Excursions are arranged regularly
Best known for its (winter sports)

Chapter 6
SERVICE WITH A SMILE

Room services

Here are some examples of room services a hotel may offer, arranged alphabetically.

BREAKFAST	Breakfast is served in your room from 7 a.m. till 10 a.m. If you wish to have breakfast in your room, ask for **Room Service** on the phone.
CLEANING	If you want to have your room cleaned extra quickly, please hang the **Cleaning** sign on the door.
DRY-CLEANING	Items handed in for dry-cleaning before 9 a.m. will be returned in the course of the same day. Please call **Room Service.**
EARLY CALL	The panel at the head of your bed contains an automatic waking device.
ELECTRICITY	There is a 220 volt and 110 volt shaving plug in the bathroom of your room.
IRONING	Please call **Room Service.**
LAUNDRY	Special laundry bags with lists are placed in your wardrobe. Washing handed in by 9.30 a.m. will be returned to you after 5.30 p.m. on the same day.
QUIET	If you wish to remain undisturbed, please hang the **Do Not Disturb** sign on your door.

Hotel English

RADIO   There is a radio in the panel at the head of your bed. You have a choice of three programmes.

RECEPTION   For all enquiries just lift your telephone receiver and you will get **Reception.**

ROOM SERVICE   If you require such assistance, just lift the telephone receiver and ask for **Room Service.**

TELEPHONE   Direct calls can be dialled straight from your room. Dial 9 for a line. You will be charged according to the call-meter in the cashier's office. Other calls may be ordered through the switchboard operator.

TV   A TV set can be installed in all rooms. You can rent a TV through **Room Service.**

Here is a series of conversations between a Receptionist and a number of hotel guests.

a.   Can I get breakfast in my room?

b.   Certainly sir. It's served in your room from 8 until 10.

a.   How do I order it?

b.   Just ask for Room Service on the phone, or I can make a note of it if you like sir.

a.   Yes, I'd like it at 8.30 tomorrow morning—that's the continental breakfast.

b.   Very good sir.

a.   I've just spilled some soup on my best dress, and we're leaving first thing the day after tomorrow. How on earth can I get it cleaned?

b.   If you hand it in for dry cleaning before 9 tomorrow morning, it'll be returned to you the same day. I can get you Room Service and arrange it now if you like madam.

a.   Oh, could you really? That would be wonderful.

a. I'll be needing an early call tomorrow—can you fix that for me?

b. There's an automatic waking device in the panel at the head of your bed. You just set it to the time you want.

---

a. I thought you had TV in all your rooms here.

b. I'm afraid not sir, but we can install one in your room.

a. Will that be extra?

b. Yes sir. Our charge for a colour TV is four Finnish marks per day.

a. Well, I'll have to ask my wife what she thinks.

b. Very good sir, and if you decide to rent one, would you please call Room Service?

---

a. (Sarcastically) Are you free to answer my question at last?

b. Yes, of course madam—as you see, we've been rather busy today.

a. So it seems. I tried to find a maid this morning, but there wasn't anyone there.

b. When you want Room Service madam, just lift the phone in your room and ask for Room Service.

a. Oh, that's how you do it—and how was I supposed to know?

Hotel English

Other services

COLD DRINKS	On each floor there are automatic drink and ice dispensers. See corridor signs.
CONFERENCE FACILITIES	**Information** will be pleased to supply you with full details. (See Chapter 9)
CREDIT CARDS	The hotel accepts Eurocard as well as American Express.
DEPARTURE	The rooms are at your disposal until 12 noon on the day of your departure. Should you require your room after that hour, kindly notify **Reception** before 10 a.m.
DEPOSITS	The hotel assumes no responsibility for money or valuables left in any of the rooms. A safe-deposit box is available free of charge. Please contact **Reception.**
GARAGE	Located in the basement. Please contact **Information** if you wish us to take care of your car.
ICE	See **Cold Drinks.**
INFORMATION	The hotel performs numerous services for its guests. For instance, you can obtain travel, sight-seeing, theatre and cinema tickets through **Information.** Just lift your phone and ask for **Information.**
RESTAURANT	(Brasserie) On the ground floor. Open weekdays: 12 noon—1 a.m. Sundays 1 p.m.—1 a.m. Set meals for guests are: **Breakfast:** 7 a.m.—10.30 a.m. **Lunch:** 12 noon—2 p.m. **Dinner:** 6.30 p.m.—8.30 p.m.
SHOESHINE SERVICE	There is a free shining machine on every floor. See corridor signs.
SOUVENIRS	The articles exhibited in the show cases may be purchased through **Reception.**
TELEX	Telexes are dealt with by **Information.**

Service With a Smile

Let's return to the Reception Desk. Here are some more requests for information.

a. Can I help you madam?
b. Is there a bank at this hotel?
a. Yes madam, the International Bank has an office on the ground floor of the hotel.
b. Is it open yet?
a. Yes madam, the bank is open from Monday to Friday from 9.30 a.m. till 3.00 p.m.
b. Thank you.

---

a. Can I still get breakfast in the brasserie?
b. Yes sir, if you hurry you can just make it—breakfast is served until 10.30.

---

a. Can I help you?
b. Do you accept credit cards here?
a. Certainly sir. We accept both Eurocards and American Express credit cards.

---

a. How soon do I have to leave my room?
b. Normally it's by 12 noon on the day of your departure.
a. Well, you see, my plane doesn't go till half past five tomorrow afternoon.
b. I see. Which room is it madam?
a. Room 577—the name is Browning.
b. Ah yes Mrs Browning. You may keep the room till 3 p.m. if you wish.
a. Oh, that's nice. Thank you very much.

Hotel English

Practice

Exercise I Answer the following questions:
1. Can I have my laundry washed at this hotel?
2. Can I get it back during the same day?
3. How can I contact the Room Service?
4. How can I dial direct?
5. How do you charge me for calls?
6. I'd like to make a phone call to New York City. What should I do?

Exercise II Fill in:
1. Washing handed in by 9 a.m. will be _____ to you after 5 p.m.
2. Please hang the Cleaning _____ on the door.
3. There is a 220 V _____ plug in the bathroom.
4. The panel at the head of your bed contains an automatic _____.
5. If you want to call Reception just lift your telephone _____.
6. When you want to make a phone call _____ 9 for a line.

Exercise III Answer the following questions using the list of services:
1. Where can I change some money?
2. Where can I have breakfast?
3. Where can I get cigarettes at this hour?
4. Can I pay my bill with my Diners' club card?
5. I've got some important papers and I wouldn't like to leave them in my room. What should I do?
6. How long can I keep my room on my departure day?
7. Where can I leave my car?
8. Where can I get some ice?
9. I'd like to go on a sight-seeing tour. Is that possible?
10. When is the restaurant open?
11. Can I get my laundry done here?
12. Where can I buy souvenirs?

Exercise IV Fill in the gaps.

1. We serve some light _____ such as hamburgers and sandwiches in the brasserie.
2. You can leave your coat at the _____ in the hotel lobby.
3. We do not _____ any credit cards.
4. Jewels, cameras and money are _____ .
5. The rooms are _____ your _____ until 3 p.m.
6. For further information, please _____ the room service.
7. The reception is responsible _____ questions regarding your reservation.
8. The operator _____ calls to your room.
9. A TV set can be _____ in all rooms.
10. Souvenirs are _____ sale _____ the shop on the ground floor.

Breakfast in the hotel room

HOTEL NEPTUNE

BREAKFAST MENU

Served in your room from 7 a.m. until 10 a.m. (service included)

CONTINENTAL BREAKFAST Fmk 7.00

Fruit Juice	Marmalade or jam
Toast, roll or sweet roll	Tea, coffee or hot chocolate
Butter	Eggs, cheese, ham or sausage at request.

ENGLISH BREAKFAST Fmk 12.00 (service included)

Hot or cold cereal	Toast and butter
Bacon, sausage and egg	Marmalade
	Tea, coffee or hot chocolate

Hotel English

Yvonne Deraine is staying at the Hotel *Neptune*. She goes to the Reception Desk and asks:

Yvonne   Can I have breakfast in my room?
Clerk   Certainly madam. Breakfast is served in your room from 7 o'clock until 10. Here is the menu.
Yvonne   Thank you. (looks at the menu) I'd like to have the Continental Breakfast.
Clerk   Yes madam. And at what time would you like it?
Yvonne   About half-past eight I think.
Clerk   8.30. Very good madam. And what kind of fruit juice would you like? We have pineapple, orange, grapefruit...
Yvonne   I think I'd like pineapple please.
Clerk   Pineapple juice. And would you prefer tea or coffee?
Yvonne   Coffee please.
Clerk   Thank you very much. Goodnight.

At 8.30 the next morning, there is a light tap at Yvonne's door.

Yvonne   Y-es... Come in.
Maid   I've brought you your breakfast madam.
Yvonne   Oh yes. Thank you. Could you put it on the desk over over there please?
Maid   Shall I pour you a cup of coffee straight away madam?
Yvonne   No thanks, I'll pour it myself in a minute.
Maid   Is there anything else madam?
Yvonne   No—no, I don't think so, thank you.

Practice

In the Hotel *Neptune*, guests can use the breakfast card to order what they want. Practise explaining the items on the card on page 65 in pairs and mark on it what is ordered.

Service With a Smile

HOTEL NEPTUNE
Breakfast card

ROOM   **TO BE SERVED AT**

                                                    O'CLOCK

PERSONS   **Please hang this card on your door**

Breakfast is also served in the Steakhouse from 7 to 10 a.m.

CONTINENTAL BREAKFAST (Service included) 9 Fmk
- ☐ COFFEE ☐ TEA ☐ HOT CHOCOLATE

Fruit Juice, Bread, Danish Pastry, Butter, Cheese, Marmalade

ENGLISH BREAKFAST (Service included) 12 Fmk
- ☐ COFFEE ☐ TEA ☐ HOT CHOCOLATE
- ☐ HAM ☐ BACON

Fruit Juice, Toast, Danish Pastry, Butter, Cheese, Marmalade

☐ EGG	☐ boiled __ min.		☐ fried	1.00
☐ HAM AND EGG	5.00	☐ MILK		1.00
☐ BACON AND EGG	5.50	☐ BUTTERMILK		1.00
☐ SCRAMBLED EGGS	4.00			
☐ PLAIN OMELETTE	4.00	☐ PLAIN YOGHOURT		2.00
☐ COFFEE	3.00	☐ PINEAPPLE YOGHOURT		2.00
☐ CAFE HAG	3.50	☐ RASPBERRY YOGHOURT		2.00
☐ TEA	2.00			
☐ HOT CHOCOLATE	3.00	☐ ORANGE JUICE		1.50
☐ OVOMALTINE	3.00	☐ GRAPEFRUIT JUICE		1.50
☐ ROLL	1.00	☐ TOMATO JUICE		1.50
☐ TOAST	1.50	☐ MINERAL WATER		2.00
☐ BUTTER	1.50	CEREALS		
☐ SWISS CHEESE	2.00	☐ OATMEAL		2.00
☐ BUTTER CHEESE	1.50	☐ FARINA		2.00
		☐ CORN FLAKES		2.00
		☐ HONEY		1.50
☐ ORANGE MARMALADE	1.00	☐ PRUNES		1.00
☐ CHERRY MARMALADE	1.00	☐ ½ GRAPEFRUIT		1.00
☐ SMOKED REINDEER	4.00	☐ FRESH FRUIT		4.00

Service charge 15%

Hotel English

Useful phrases

Breakfast can be served in your room
We can install a TV in your room
Please hang the card on your door
Just lift the telephone receiver to get Reception
Direct calls can be dialled from your room
I'll arrange for that to be done right away
There are automatic drinks dispensers in the corridors
Will there be anything else?

Chapter 7
ON THE PHONE
Telephone conversations

Hotel
Operator   *Neptune* Hotel. Good afternoon.
Man   I'd like to order a room for next Thursday.
Operator   Yes sir. I'll put you through to Reception. . . you're through.

Reception
Clerk   Hotel Reception—can I help you?
Man   Yes, I'd like a single room with bath for next Thursday.
Clerk   What name is it please?
Man   Remington—Charles Remington.
Clerk   And how long would you be staying Mr Remington?
Man   Three—possibly four days.
Clerk   Very good Mr Remington. I've booked you a single room with bath for three nights from Thursday, October 14th.
Man   Fine.
Clerk   And we look forward to seeing you then sir.

Operator   *Neptune* Hotel. Good morning.
Woman   Could I speak to Jimmy Slater?
Operator   What name was that please?
Woman   Slater: S-L-A-T-E-R.
Operator   Thank you. I'll put you through to Mr Slater's room straight away.

Hotel English

Operator	Neptune Hotel. Good evening.
Man	Good evening. Can you put me through to the Manager please?
Operator	Yes sir. Trying to connect you.
Man	Thank you
Operator	You're through caller. Go ahead.
Secretary	Manager's office. Can I help you?
Man	I'd like to speak to the Manager please.
Secretary	Who's calling please?
Man	Tell him it's Mr Selby.
Secretary	I'm sorry, I didn't quite catch that. Did you say Felby?
Man	SELBY. 'S' for sugar.
Secretary	Hold the line please...... I'm sorry, he's busy at the moment. Can I take a message?
Man	No, it's all right. I'll try again later.

Spelling on the phone

You must also be prepared to spell things in English on the phone.

When spelling the same letter twice, British people usually say "double B", "double E", as in RUBBER: R—U—double B—E—R, or FEED: F—double E—D, but Americans don't.
Telephone numbers:
O is pronounced ou (Br.), zero (Am.). The British say "double 7" in a number like 6774, but Americans say six-seven-seven-four.

This is the British system:

A	for Andrew	J	for Jack	S	for Sugar
B	Benjamin	K	King	T	Tommy
C	Charlie	L	Lucy	U	Uncle
D	David	M	Mary	V	Victory
E	Edward	N	Nellie	W	William
F	Frederick	O	Oliver	X	Xmas
G	George	P	Peter	Y	Yellow
H	Harry	Q	Queenie	Z	Zebra
I	Isaac	R	Robert		

My name is Philip Binham. Philip: P for Peter, H for Harry, I for Isaac, L for Lucy, I for Isaac, P for Peter. Binham: B for Benjamin, I for Isaac, N for Nellie, H for Harry, A for Andrew, M for Mary.

On the Phone

Practice

Exercise I   Practise the following situations as telephone conversations:

1. The operator at the Hotel *Neptune* answers the phone. The caller wants to book a double room. The operator transfers the call to Reception. The caller wants the room from February 1 to February 3 and asks for details about the room, facilities, charges etc.

2. The caller wants to speak to the Manager but his secretary says he's busy so takes the message that the Manager should call 55 88 22 when he returns.

3. The caller wants to leave a message for a guest at the hotel and is put through to Reception. The line is very bad, however, so the Receptionist takes the caller's number, calls back and takes the message.

Exercise II   Fill in:

A: Hotel *Neptune*, good morning.

B: This is Mr Jones, good morning. _____ Mrs Miller please.

A: _____ I'll check if Mrs Miller is in.

A: _____ she isn't in just now. Can I leave her a _____

B: Certainly. Tell her that I'll _____ at 3 o'clock.

Exercise III   Change the following sentences as in the example:

Tell him I shall be in the cafeteria.

He left a message to say that he would be in the cafeteria.

1. She will contact the travel agency.
2. I have left the car at the service station.
3. They will be attending the conference in the afternoon.
4. He will come to the Lobby Bar at 8 p.m.

Hotel English

5   They have planned to spend the evening at home.
6   The maid has found his passport in the wardrobe.
7   The porter has taken the suitcases to the wrong room.
8   He will return the road and rail timetable tomorrow.
9   She forgot to endorse the cheque.
10 I shall not require breakfast on Sunday morning.

Exercise IV   Express the following in a different way using the word(s) in brackets:

1   The line is busy. Please wait. (engaged/hold on)
2   I am connecting you. (put through)
3   Mr Jones is not here. Shall I ask him to telephone you? (call back)
4   I am sorry it is taking a long time. (keep/waiting)
5   What is your name (who/calling?)
6   The line went dead while we were talking. (cut off)
7   Say that again please. (mind/repeat)
8   I will tell him what you said. (pass/message)

Useful phrases

Who's calling please?
Hold the line please
One moment please. I'll put you through
Trying to connect you
I'm sorry, the number's engaged. Will you hold?
You're through now
I'm sorry to keep you waiting
Can I take a message?
I'm sorry but I didn't quite catch that
Would you mind repeating that please?
Can you spell that for me?

On the Phone

It's a bad line. I can't hear you clearly
I think we were cut off
Thank you for calling
I'm sorry, he's busy at the moment. Can you call back?

He's { on the phone / gone out to lunch / at a meeting }   He'll be back { in a minute / after lunch / next week }

On the phone has two meanings:

1. Are you on the phone?—This means, do you have a telephone, and if so, what's your number?

2. If you went into an office and asked to speak to Mr Jones, his secretary might say "He's on the phone at the moment. Could you wait a minute please?"—meaning: He is speaking on the telephone.

Some words you need when making a phone call abroad:

a long distance call
a trunk call
I want to make a **long distance call** to Paris.

I want to make **a person to person call** to Mr Smith.
I want to make **a station to station call** to Sheraton, Stockholm.

I want to make **a reverse charge call** (Br.)/**a collect call** (Am.) to my parents.

The number is 5245, area code/routing number 90.
I want to cancel my call to Paris.

Chapter 8
HOW TO GET THERE

Asking the way

One of the services that a good hotel staff will offer is to help guests to find various places and services outside the hotel itself.

Now look at the map on page 74. A member of the hotel staff is standing on the steps outside the hotel and giving directions. Follow the answers with the help of your map.

a. Excuse me, could you tell me the way to the railway station please?

b. Yes, go straight down this street here, turn left and then take the first on your right.

a. I'm looking for the Catholic Church, can you help me?

b. You go along this street here, turn sharp right and it's about 200 yards along on the other side of the road. You can't miss it.

a. Can you tell me where the nearest travel agency is please?

b. Yes, go straight down this street here, turn right into George Street, go straight along until you come to Union Street and it's straight in front of you, opposite the chemist's on the corner.

a. I would like to send a telex. Is that possible?

b. Well, you could try the Post Office. Go up this street, turn left into Churchill Street and go straight along until you come to Union Street and you'll find it on the corner. It's a big yellow building.

How to Get There

a. I would like to change some traveller's cheques. Can you tell me where the nearest bank or currency exchange office is please?

b. Well, there's a bank on the corner opposite the railway station. First left, then left again. The entrance is in Crown Street.

a. Where do they sell tin-openers and corkscrews?

b. Your best bet is Beal's department store on the corner opposite the Post Office. First left, cross the road and it's right in front of you.

a. Is there an all-night chemist's in the centre of town?

b. Well, there is a chemist's on the corner of Union Street and George Street, but I don't know if it's open after 5.30.

Hotel English

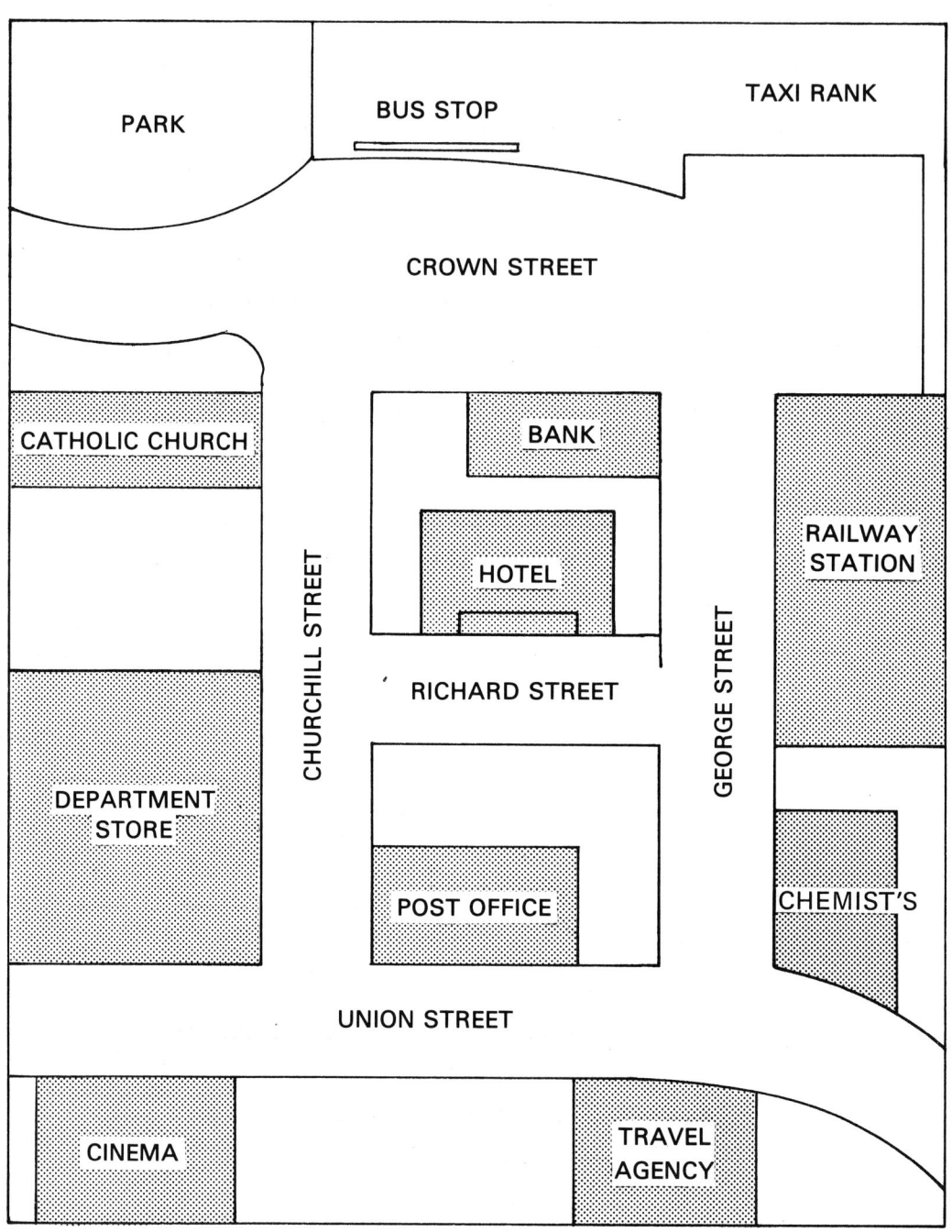

How to Get There

Practice

Here are some questions to answer. You are standing outside the railway station.

1. Can you tell me the way to the bus stop?
2. Can you direct me to the cinema please?
3. I'm looking for the post office. Can you help me please?

Now practise some more questions and answers in pairs.

Complete the questions in list A and the answers in list B to make dialogues of your own:

a. Could you tell me where .... is?
   the way to .... ?
   Where can I find a .... ?
   How far is the nearest .... ?
   Is there a .... nearby?
   You'll find .... { on your left.
   on your right.
   right opposite.
   on the corner.

b. It's about a .... minute's walk.
   Your best bet is to ....
   Carry straight on until you see .... and then ....

Look at the map of part of central London and answer the following questions. Imagine you are standing at the Victoria Green Line Coach station on the corner of Buckingham Palace Road and Eccleston Bridge (marked with an arrow).

Excuse me, can you tell me the way to:

1. Buckingham Palace?
2. The Hyde Park bandstand? (1C)
3. Park Lane hotel? (2C)
4. Victoria Square? (2D)
5. Wilton Row? (1C)

Practise some more questions and answers in pairs.

75

Hotel English

How to Get There

Travelling by sea

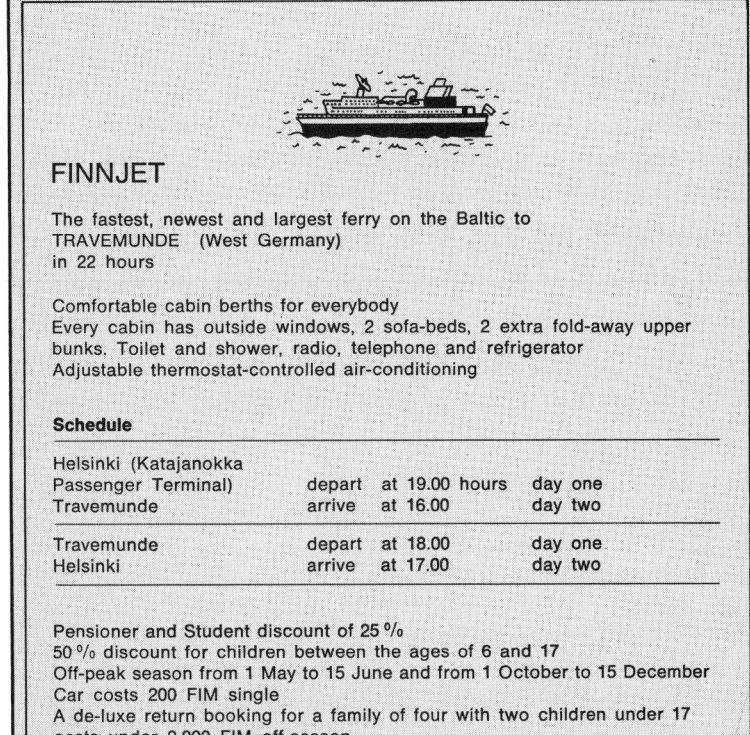

FINNJET

The fastest, newest and largest ferry on the Baltic to
TRAVEMUNDE (West Germany)
in 22 hours

Comfortable cabin berths for everybody
Every cabin has outside windows, 2 sofa-beds, 2 extra fold-away upper bunks. Toilet and shower, radio, telephone and refrigerator
Adjustable thermostat-controlled air-conditioning

Schedule

Helsinki (Katajanokka Passenger Terminal)	depart at 19.00 hours	day one
Travemunde	arrive at 16.00	day two
Travemunde	depart at 18.00	day one
Helsinki	arrive at 17.00	day two

Pensioner and Student discount of 25 %
50 % discount for children between the ages of 6 and 17
Off-peak season from 1 May to 15 June and from 1 October to 15 December
Car costs 200 FIM single
A de-luxe return booking for a family of four with two children under 17 costs under 2 000 FIM off-season
Meals are not included in the price of the tickets
Phone your local travel agent for more details

Practice

Answer the following enquiries using the Finnjet brochure:

1. Are there any direct sailings from Finland to Germany?
2. When does the boat leave?
3. Where does it leave from?
4. How much would it be for a car return?
5. Are there any reductions for students?
6. Are meals included in the price of tickets?
7. What are the cabins like?
8. When does the off-peak season run?

Hotel English

Travelling by air

Look at the Helsinki—Budapest schedule, then at this enquiry.

a. Could you tell me about flights to Budapest please?
b. Certainly sir. There's a Finnair flight that leaves Helsinki at 9.20 via Copenhagen arriving in Budapest at 12.20.
a. Does that go every day?
b. No, only on Mondays and Fridays.
a. I would like to go in the middle of the week. Is there anything else? A non-stop flight, for instance?
b. Yes, on Thursdays and Sundays there is a Malév flight non-stop to Budapest leaving at 18.00 and arriving 19.35 local time.
a. What on earth is Malév?
b. The Hungarian Airlines.
a. And what planes do they use?
b. They fly Soviet planes, the Tupolev 134.
a. Is that first class?
b. No, I'm afaid not, only economy class. But after the 5 March there is a later flight leaving Helsinki at 20.30 arriving at 21.55.
a. Fine. Well, I think that would suit me. How can I reserve a seat on that flight?
b. Just a minute sir, I'll get the number for you. Yes, here we are. Finnair reservations 473311. It's ringing now sir.

Now look at the instructions on how to use the timetable and prepare to answer the following enquiries:

Could you tell me about flights to Athens please?
I would like to fly to East Berlin, can you help me?
Can I fly to Boston on Sunday?
What time does the 2 p.m. flight get into Brussels?
Are the flights to Amsterdam non-stop?
How many flights are there to Bangkok?

How to Get There

HOW TO USE THIS TIMETABLE

```
Airport name
Only given when a city has more than one airport

          HELSINKI – PARIS (Orly)
26Sep –          1 2 3 4 5 6 7     0850 1200     AY 873 D9S  FY           via BRU
       – 25Sep  1 2 3 4 5 6 7     0850 1300     AY 873 D9S  FY           via BRU
        26Sep –         1 2 3 4 5 6 7  1400 1805     AY LH 823 CVS FY    1535 FRA 1655   LH 114 A3B⊕FY
                – 25Sep 1 2 3 4 5 6 7  1400 1905     AY LH 823 CVS FY    1535 FRA 1655   LH 114 A3B⊕FY

                        Days of operation           Flight information              Transfer point and timings
Validity of flights or connections                   – Airline codes                 – Arrival time to transfer point
If blank, the flights will operate                   – Flight number                 – City/airport code
throughout the season                                – Aircraft type                 – Departure time from transfer point
                        Times of departure           – Class of service
                        and arrival                                                  Connecting flight information
                                                                                     – Airline codes
                                                                                     – Flight number
                                                                                     – Aircraft type
                                                                                     – Class of service
```

EXPLANATION OF SIGNS AND SYMBOLS

AA = American Airlines	AGP = Malaga	707 = Boeing 707				
AC = Air Canada	AMS = Amsterdam	727 = Boeing 727				
AF = Air France	ARN = Arlanda (Stockholm)	737 = Boeing 737				
AY = Finnair	BCN = Barcelona	747 = Boeing 747				
AZ = Alitalia	BKK = Bangkok	AB3 = A300B Airbus				
BA = British Airways	BRU = Brussels	B11 = BAC One-Eleven				
BR = British Caledonian Airways	BUD = Budapest	CV4 = Convair Metropolitan				
BU = Braathens S.A.F.E.	CPH = Copenhagen	CRB = Super Caravelle				
DL = Delta Air Lines	DUS = Dusseldorf	CRV = Caravelle				
EA = Eastern Air Lines	EWR = Newark (New York)	D6B = Douglas DC-6B				
EI = Aer Lingus	FCO = Fiumicino (Rome)	D8S = Douglas DC-8-62/63				
FI = Icelandair	FRA = Frankfurt	D9F = Douglas DC-9 Freighter				
HN = NLM – Dutch Airlines	GOT = Gothenburg	D9S = Douglas DC-9-30/40/50				
IB = Iberia	HAM = Hamburg	D10 = Douglas DC-10				
IF = Interflug	HEL = Helsinki	DC8 = Douglas DC-8				
IT = Air Inter	JFK = J. F. Kennedy (New York)	DC9 = Douglas DC-9				
JL = Japan Air Lines	LEJ = Leipzig	DAM = Dassault Mercure				
JU = Jugoslovenski Aerotransport	LGA = La Guardia (New York)	DHT = De Havilland Twin Otter				
KL = KLM Royal Dutch Airlines	LHR = Heathrow (London)	FKF = Fokker F-27 Friendship				
KR = Kar-Air	LIN = Linate (Milan)	IL6 = Ilyushin IL-62				
LG = Luxair	LUX = Luxembourg	IL8 = Ilyushin IL-18				
LH = Lufthansa German Airlines	MAN = Manchester	L10 = Lockheed 1011 TriStar				
LO = LOT – Polish Airlines	MHQ = Mariehamn	TU3 = Tupolev TU-134				
LZ = Balkan	ORY = Orly (Paris)	TU5 = Tupolev TU-154				
MA = Malev	OSL = Oslo	TRD = Trident				
NA = National Airlines	POR = Pori					
NW = Northwest Orient Airlines	PRG = Prague	1 = Monday				
OA = Olympic Airways	SVO = Sheremetyevo (Moscow)	2 = Tuesday				
OK = Ceskoslovenske Aerolinie	SXT = Schönefeld (Berlin)	3 = Wednesday				
OS = Austrian Airlines	TAS = Tashkent	4 = Thursday				
PA = Pan American Airways	TKU = Turku	5 = Friday				
RO = Tarom	UME = Umeå	6 = Saturday				
SK = Scandinavian Airlines	VAA = Vaasa	7 = Sunday				
SN = Sabena	VIE = Vienna	● = Next day				
SR = Swissair	WAW = Warsaw					
SU = Aeroflot – Soviet Airlines	YMX = Mirabel (Montreal)	F = First class				
TK = THY Turkish Airlines	YUL = Dorval (Montreal)	Y = Economy class				
TP = Transportes Aereos Portugueses	ZRH = Zurich	U = Air Shuttle				
TW = Trans World Airlines		CG = Cargo				
UA = United Airlines						

79

Hotel English

INTERNATIONAL SERVICES

Validity From – To	Days	Dep	Arr	Flight	A/C	Class	Transfer information Arr City Dep	Flight	A/C	Class
HELSINKI – AARHUS										
	1 5	0920	1205	AY 753	CRB	Y	1000 CPH 1135	SK 235	D9S	Y
	1 2 3 4 5 6 7	1225	1625	AY 813	CRB	FY	1345 CPH 1555	SK 239	D9S	Y
	1 2 3 4 5 6 7	1820	2040	AY 863	D9S	FY	1900 CPH 2010	SK 243	D9S	Y
HELSINKI – AMSTERDAM										
	1 2 3 4 5 6 7	0800	1015	AY 853	CRB	FY	via HAM			
	1 2 3 4 6	0925	1140	AY 841	CRB	FY	via GOT			
	5 7	0925	1140	AY 841	CRB	Y	via GOT			
	4	1035	1315	AY 101	D10	FY	via CPH			
	– 28Nov 1 5	1155	1315	AY 103	D10	FY	NONSTOP			
	12Dec – 1 5	1155	1315	AY 103	D10	FY	NONSTOP			
	5Dec only 1	1155	1315	AY 103	D10	FY	NONSTOP			
	2Dec – 9Dec 5	1155	1315	AY 103	D8S	Y	NONSTOP			
HELSINKI – ATHENS										
	1 2 3 4 5 6 7	0710	1325	AY 821	D9S	FY	0845 FRA 0935	LH 310	727	FY
	4 7	0730	1405	AYAZ 865	CRB	Y	1030 FCO 1120	OA 234	727	FY
	– 10Dec 2 6	0825	1450	AY 761	CRB	Y	1105 VIE 1135	OS 871	D9S	FY
	4Mar – 2 6	0825	1450	AY 761	CRB	Y	1105 VIE 1135	OS 871	D9S	FY
	17Dec – 25Feb 6	0825	1450	AY 761	CRB	Y	1105 VIE 1135	OS 871	D9S	FY
HELSINKI – BANGKOK										
	1	1435●0705		AY 902	D8S	Y	via TAS			
HELSINKI – BARCELONA										
	6	1000	1415	AY 893	D9S	Y	via LUX			
	1 2 3 4 5 6 7	0710	1215	AY 821	D9S	FY	0845 FRA 1015	LH 170	737	FY
	1 2 3 4 5 6 7	0850	1335	AY 873	D9S	FY	1030 BRU 1140	SN 691	737	Y
	5	0945	1420	AYAZ 867	CRB	Y	1200 LIN 1250	AZ 358	D9S	FY
HELSINKI – BASEL										
	1 2 3 4 5 7	1820	2250	AY 863	D9S	FY	2110 ZRH 2220	SR 437	D9S	FY
	6	1820	2250	AY 863	D9S	FY	2110 ZRH 2220	SR 970	D9S	FY
HELSINKI – BELGRADE										
	1 2 3 5	0710	1200	AY 821	D9S	FY	0845 FRA 1005	LH 360	737	FY
	2 6	0825	1535	AY 761	CRB	Y	1105 VIE 1425	OS 821	D9S	FY
	– 9Mar 4 7	0920	1420	AY 771	DC9	Y	1035 SXF 1140	JU 381	D9S	Y
	19Mar – 4 7	0920	1420	AY 771	DC9	Y	1035 SXF 1140	JU 381	D9S	Y
	1	1025	1620	AY 763	CRB	Y	1120 WAW 1450	JU 341	D9S	Y
	1 4	1400	2050	AYLH 823	D9S	FY	1535 FRA 1815	JU 357	D9S	Y
	2 3 5 6 7	1400	2050	AYLH 823	D9S	FY	1535 FRA 1815	JU 353	D9S	Y
HELSINKI – BERGEN										
	1 2 3 4 5 6 7	0805	1110	AY 791	D9S	Y	0925 OSL 1025	SK 307	D9S	Y
	1 2 3 4 5 7	1900	2145	AY 797	CRB	FY	1925 OSL 2100	SK 317	D9S	Y
HELSINKI – BERLIN (Schönefeld)										
	– 9Mar 4	0920	1035	AY 771	DC9	Y	NONSTOP			
	23Mar – 4	0920	1035	AY 771	DC9	Y	NONSTOP			
	– 5Mar 7	0920	1035	AY 771	CRB	Y	NONSTOP			
	19Mar – 7	0920	1035	AY 771	CRB	Y	NONSTOP			
	2 6	1425	1535	IF 701	TU3	Y	NONSTOP			
	3 5 7	1225	1550	AY 813	CRB	FY	1345 CPH 1455	SK 737	DC9	Y
HELSINKI – BERLIN WEST (Tegel)										
	1 2 3 4 5 6 7	0800	1025	AY 853	CRB	FY	0855 HAM 0945	PA 602	727	Y
	5	1730	2015	LH 027	727	FY	1830 HAM 1935	PA 616	727	Y
	1 2 3 4 5 6 7	1730	2135	LH 027	727	FY	1830 HAM 2055	PA 618	727	Y
HELSINKI – BOSTON										
	4	1035	2123	AY 101	D10	FY	1605 JFK 2015	TW 042	L10	FY
	1 5	1155	2123	AY 103	D10	FY	1605 JFK 2015	TW 042	L10	FY
	28Dec only 3	1400	2123	AY 105	D8S	Y	1605 JFK 2015	TW 042	L10	FY
	21 Dec only 3	1430	2123	AY 111	D8S	Y	1740 JFK 2015	TW 042	L10	FY
	6	1430	2123	AY 111	D10	FY	1740 JFK 2015	TW 042	L10	FY
HELSINKI – BRUSSELS										
	1 2 3 4 5 6 7	0850	1030	AY 873	D9S	FY	NONSTOP			
	1 2 3 4 5 6 7	1400	1750	AYLH 823	D9S	FY	1535 FRA 1650	LH 104	737	FY
HELSINKI – BUCHAREST (Otopeni)										
	1 4 6 7	0710	1535	AY 821	D9S	FY	0845 FRA 1210	RO 216	B11	Y
	2 3 5	0710	1725	AY 821	D9S	FY	0845 FRA 1245	LH 370	737	FY
	2	0825	1440	AY 761	CRB	Y	1105 VIE 1205	OS 841	D9S	FY
	5	0920	1705	AY 753	CRB	Y	1220 BUD 1505	RO 226	B11	Y
HELSINKI – BUDAPEST										
	1 5	0920	1220	AY 753	CRB	Y	via CPH			
	– 26Feb 4 7	1800	1935	MA 743	TU3	Y	NONSTOP			
	2Mar – 4	1800	1935	MA 743	TU3	Y	NONSTOP			
	7	2030	2155	MA 743	TU5	FY	NONSTOP			

80

How to Get There

Time on your hands

Asking the Time

	Replies:
What's the time?	It's ....
What time is it please?	It's just coming up to
What time do you make it?	....
	I make it ....
	It's just gone ....

Note the different ways of saying certain times:

    6.00: six o'clock/six a.m.
    6.05: five (minutes) past six/six oh five
    6.15: a quarter past six/six fifteen
    6.25: twenty five (minutes) past six/six twenty five
    6.30: half past six/six thirty
    6.40: twenty (minutes) to seven/six forty
    6.45: a quarter to seven/six forty five
    6.56: four minutes to seven/six fifty six

In the USA "after" is used instead of "past" and "of" instead of "to"

The twenty-four hour clock is commonly used in travel timetables where times are read as follows:

    06.00 oh six hundred hours
    10.30 ten thirty
    12.00 twelve hundred hours/midday/noon
    14.45 fourteen forty-five
    19.00 nineteen hundred hours
    23.05 twenty-three oh five
    24.00 twenty-four hundred hours/midnight

Practice with the following times first using the normal system and secondly the twenty-four hour clock:

    05.17 11.30 13.20 14.05 15.37 15.45 17.40
    18.15 19.19 20.00 21.55 23.59 24.00 00.35

Chapter 9
CONGRESS FACILITIES

Congress facilities offered by a hotel

Here is a conversation at the Front Desk:

a. Good morning, sir. Can I help you?
b. I'd like some information on the prices for renting equipment and personnel for our congress.
a. Certainly sir. I have the list right here.
b. Well, we shall need an overhead projector for three days, a slide projector only on the Monday and then it would be handy to have a tape recorder for a couple of days.
a. The overhead is 35 marks a day, so that is 105 marks, the slide projector 25, that makes 130, and the tape recorder is 30 marks a day, so that would make a total of 190 marks altogether sir.
b. What is that in dollars?
a. Approximately 50 dollars sir.
b. That's a bit steep. Say, do you have any of this closed circuit TV business—how much does that work out at?
a. We have some brand-new Japanese equipment which costs around 45 dollars for 3 hours. But of course you have the advantage of both picture and sound.
b. Yeah, that sounds great. Sign me up for that and thanks for the suggestion.
a. Not at all. Glad to be of assistance.

Congress Facilities

Besides its normal hotel services, the Hotel Neptune also offers congress facilities. Here is what they offer:

**HOTEL NEPTUNE
INTERNATIONAL CONGRESS CENTRE**

Price list for equipment and services

Valid from 01.06.1976

overhead projector	35 Fmk/day
slide projector	25 Fmk/day
epidiascope	50 Fmk/day
8 mm film projector (optical)	30 Fmk/day
16 mm film projector (magnetic)	60 Fmk/hour
tape-recorder	30 Fmk/day
record-player	15 Fmk/day
closed circuit TV equipment	175 Fmk/3 hours
Projectionist	35 Fmk/hour
Guides (in Finnish)	25 Fmk/hour
Guides (in foreign languages)	65 Fmk/hour
Interpreters (consecutive)	approximately 100 DM/day
Interpreters (simultaneous)	approximately 150 DM/day + travelling expenses
Messenger boys	10—15 Fmk/hour

Practice

Look at the price list and answer the following enquiries:

1. Could you tell me the cost of hiring guides who speak foreign languages please?
2. What kind of film projectors do you rent out?
3. What do messenger boys cost these days?
4. Could you tell me the approximate cost in £s of hiring 3 simultaneous interpreters for a two-day seminar we are arranging?
5. If I hire a film projector from you, does that include the cost of the projectionist?
6. Do you have such a thing as an epidiascope?

Hotel English

Here is a conversation about congress facilities:

Bamforth   The name is Bamforth—Congress Consultants Ltd. Here is my card. I'm here to check the equipment we ordered for the International Conference of Journalists to be held at your hotel tomorrow.

Manager   Certainly sir. Come right this way. I'll take you to the auditorium and we can both check the equipment on the spot. It's just along the corridor here. Lovely weather for the time of year, don't you think.

Bamforth   Yes, indeed. I do love the spring. Your hotel's quite new I understand.

Manager   Yes, it is. Completed last year as a matter of fact. Ah. Here we are. After you sir. The overhead project is on this table here.

Bamforth   I see. Do you have some extra cloth pens in different colours? Our speakers are very particular about that.

Manager   Certainly. I'll order a complete range.

Bamforth   By the way, this slide projector doesn't seem to be working. I think it needs a new bulb.

Manager   I'll attend to that right away. No, just a minute. It's not necessary. It wasn't plugged in properly.

Bamforth   Now let me see—the tape recorder has an empty spool, but the film projector doesn't seem to have an empty reel.

Manager   No, that's in my office. The Deputy Manager borrowed it. I'll make a note of it.

Bamforth   And do you have an extra magazine for the slide projector?

Manager   Yes, there are two available in this drawer here.

Bamforth   You have a couple of electric typewriters on the desk over there, but is there an adequate supply of typing and carbon paper I wonder.

Manager   My secretary will be up in a minute with all the stationery, including the pencils, note-pads, folders, name boards and last but not least the all-important gavel.

Bamforth   We shall also need a notice board in addition to the normal bulletin board in the foyer.

Congress Facilities

Manager   There is a small one over here with a spare box of drawing pins on this shelf where we keep the chalk and the pointer.

Bamforth   Well, I think that is everything. You have been most efficient. Is there anything we have forgotten, do you think?

Manager   We could perhaps just test out the microphone and the amplifier, just in case. There's nothing more annoying than beginning the conference with a high-pitched whistle.

Bamforth   You're quite right. That reminds me. Is there a light on the lectern and how do we turn the lights down when we're showing the slides?

Manager   There is a dimmer switch over here by the door and I can have an extra light fitted to the lectern for you.

Bamforth   Excellent. Thank you very much indeed. You have been most helpful.

Practice

What things did Mr Bamforth check? Run through the check-list on page 86. Did he *forget* anything?

Imagine you are the Manager of the hotel. Tell him what things he should still check.

Hotel English

Technical equipment checklist

checklist.				
☐ blackboard	☐ chalk	☐ pointer	☐ duster	
☐ flip-chart	☐ cloth pens			
☐ overhead/ projector	☐ transparencies	☐ spare bulb		
☐ slide projector	☐ extra cartridge/ for slides	☐ remote control/ system		
☐ projection/ screen	☐ epidiascope			
☐ film projector/ 8/16 mm	☐ optical or/ magnetic sound	☐ empty reel		
☐ tape-recorder	☐ spare spool	☐ microphone	☐ tape	
☐ PA-system	☐ amplifier	☐ microphone	☐ loud-speakers	
☐ simultaneous/ interpreting/ equipment	☐ earphone sets	☐ 4 channels		
☐ lighting	☐ dimmer	☐ lectern light	☐ spotlights	
☐ acoustics	☐ ventilation			
☐ air-conditioning				
☐ number of/ chairs				
☐ closed circuit/ TV	☐ videotape/ recorder	☐ mixer	☐ monitor	☐ camera
☐ photocopying	☐ duplicating			
☐ typewriter	☐ typing paper	☐ carbon paper	☐ eraser	
☐ notice board	☐ drawing pins	☐ paper clips	☐ stapler	
☐ pencils	☐ gavel	☐ note-pads	☐ name boards	☐ folders

Congress Facilities

Exercise I Fill in the gaps using some of the words below:

tape recorder, technician, interpreter, screen, air-conditioning, photocopy, transparencies, microphone, acoustics.

1 I need some _____ for the overhead projector.
2 We have got a film projector but we haven't got a _____ who could show the film.
3 It's very hot in this room, I don't think the _____ is working.
4 I want to listen to his speech later on, have you got a _____ ?
5 I can't operate these machines myself, I think we need a _____ .
6 This room has excellent _____ , you can hear everything even at the back of the room.
7 We have three British lecturers so we need an _____ to translate what they say.
8 Could you please take a _____ of this text?
9 Please test the _____ before the lecture starts.

Exercise II Fill in the prepositions when necessary:

1 I want some information _____ your room rates.
2 I need this projector _____ 4 days.
3 This epidiascope costs 50 Fmk _____ day.
4 The conference will take place _____ the Hotel *Neptune*.
5 We'll contact you again _____ next week.
6 Do you have cloth pens _____ different colours?
7 I think we'll ge them _____ Thursday morning.
8 How do you turn the lights _____ when showing the slides?
9 I bought those tapes _____ two years ago.

Hotel English

Exercise III Study the conference facilities at the Hotel *Arctic* and answer the following questions in pairs:

HOTEL ARCTIC

Accommodation
Rooms 79
Beds 200
Rooms with all amenities

Congress Facilities

	guests
The Old Casino Restaurant	350
Gymnasium	150
Conference Room	60
Sunshine Room	40
Bar	30
Library	20

Several group work rooms of various sizes

Technical Facilities
Recording equipment • Overhead projectors
16 mm film projector • Slide projectors
Copying service • Typing service • Telex
Flip-charts • Blackboards
No charge for use of congress equipment
Videotape equipment can be ordered

Services
Restaurant seats 230 • Night club
Leisure rooms • Sauna
Swimming pool • Gymnasium
Tennis court • Sports equipment can be hired

1. How many people can you accommodate?
2. Have all the rooms a private bathroom?
3. What kind of meeting facilities are there?
4. Can I show 16 mm films and slides there?
5. What other meeting equipment have you got?
6. Do you have closed circuit TV equipment?
7. How about restaurant facilities?
8. What recreational facilities do you have?
9. Could I have the full postal address of the hotel please?

Congress Facilities

Types of meeting

SEMINAR — Usually a group sharing experiences in a particular field with an expert discussion leader. Attendance generally 30 persons or less.

WORKSHOP — Usually a general session with groups of participants assisting each other to gain new knowledge. Attendance generally no more than 30—35 participants.

CLINIC — Usually small groups, but may have general sessions where experts provide most of the tuition in one particular subject.

CONFERENCE — Usually general sessions and face-to-face groups planning, fact-finding and problem-solving.

FORUM — A panel discussion or presentation by experts in a given field with an opportunity for audience participation.

SYMPOSIUM — Usually a panel discussion or presentation by experts in a given field before a large audience. Some audience participation, less than a forum.

PANEL — Two or more speakers each stating their viewpoints. The discussion is led by a chairman.

LECTURE — A formal presentation by an expert, sometimes followed by audience participation.

COLLOQUIUM — A programme where the participants determine the matter to be discussed. Leaders then construct the programme around the problems that come up most frequently.

CONGRESS — A large meeting or series of meetings of experts in a given field. Often with international participation.

Hotel English

Practice

You are the Hotel Manager. Look at the rates for congress facilities, and answer the following questions:

1 How much do you charge for the use of your auditorium for a) the whole day, b) the afternoon only?
2 How much do you charge for conference equipment in the auditorium?
3 Is it possible to get photocopies?
4 I'd like to hire some rooms for group work. What are your prices?
5 Do you charge anything for the equipment we need for group work?
6 We need a conference room for a couple of hours. How much do you charge for that?
7 Have you facilities for using closed circuit TV?
8 Can you arrange interpreters for our conference and is that included in the price?
9 Is it possible to hire your nightclub for private use?

Rates for Congress Facilities

Premises	Hire if at least ⅓ of group lives in hotel		Other customers		Free Services	Chargeable services
	under 4 hours	all day	under 4 hours	all day		
Auditorium	$500	$800	$700	$950	conference equipment fixed AV equipment conference secretary conference organizers	closed circuit TV interpreting equipment copying service extra AV equipment
Conference rooms	$100	$175	$175	$250	fixed AV equipment conference secretary conference organizers	closed circuit TV interpreting equipment copying service extra AV equipment
Group work rooms	$20 per hour (max. $100 per day)	$100	$30 per hour (max. $150 per day)	$150	conference secretary conference organizers normal group work requirements	closed circuit TV copying service extra AV equipment
Big conference hall	$250	$350	$350	$500	fixed AV equipment conference secretary conference organizers	closed circuit TV interpreting equipment copying service extra AV equipment
Night club	$150	$300	$250	$500	conference secretary conference organizers	fixed sound and video equipment other equipment needed

We reserve the right to make changes in prices
All service fees are included in prices

Hotel English

A conference questionnaire

Here is an example of a questionnaire that a hotel might send as part of a survey to conference organizers.

NAME _____
TITLE _____
COMPANY/ASSOCIATION _____
ADDRESS _____
TELEPHONE _____

1. How many hotel rooms does your major conference require?
   under 50 ☐ 50—99 ☐ 100—199 ☐ 200—499 ☐ 500 plus ☐

2. How may days does your major conference last?
   1 day ☐ 1—3 days ☐ 3—5 days ☐ over 5 days ☐

3. Do you encourage pre- and post-conference trips for your delegates?
   yes ☐ no ☐

4. In what month of the year is your conference held? _____

5. Where would you consider holding your next conference?
   UK ☐ EEC Countries ☐ Mediterranean ☐ Scandinavia ☐
   North America ☐ Caribbean ☐ Latin America ☐ Asia ☐
   Africa ☐ Australia ☐ New Zealand ☐

6. What kind of venue would you consider?
   Conference centres ☐ Hotels ☐ Universities ☐

7. Preferred city/country _____
   Novelty venue _____

8. Do you require specialized help for your conference?
   audio-visual aids ☐ display equipment ☐
   multi-language interpretation ☐ exhibition hall ☐
   resort facilities ☐ airport hotel location ☐

9. Do you request group airline and hotel rates for your delegates?
   _____

10. How many minor conferences do you plan a year? _____
    What is the average number of delegates at these minor conferences? _____

THANK YOU FOR YOUR HELP

Congress Facilities

Arranging a conference on board ship

Are You Planning an Important Conference or Congress?

*Remember that the in-convention is unconventional
Why not hold your conferences and meetings at sea?*

Whatever you call it, a conference, a convention, a symposium, meeting, debate, product launch, sales talk, AGM or seminar, we can cope with it. Our multi-purpose conference centre has seating for 400. I can be used either as one big conference hall or as several smaller rooms divided up by soundproof folding partitions. Each seat in the main conference hall is equipped with a writing table, and an intercom device consisting of a loud-speaker and microphone for use during debates.

We have the most modern conference equipment available on the high seas. This includes full projection equipment—16 and 35 mm projectors, closed circuit TV and simultaneous interpretation facilities for up to eight languages.

Telex and radio keep you in touch with your company whatever it is. We also offer secretial assitance from our specially-trained, multi-lingual staff.

Best of all: There is no charge for the hire of our Conference Centre.

Many well-known companies have already made their advance bookings. Get in touch with us and we'll be only too pleased to help you with your next conference.

Hotel English

Plan of facilities

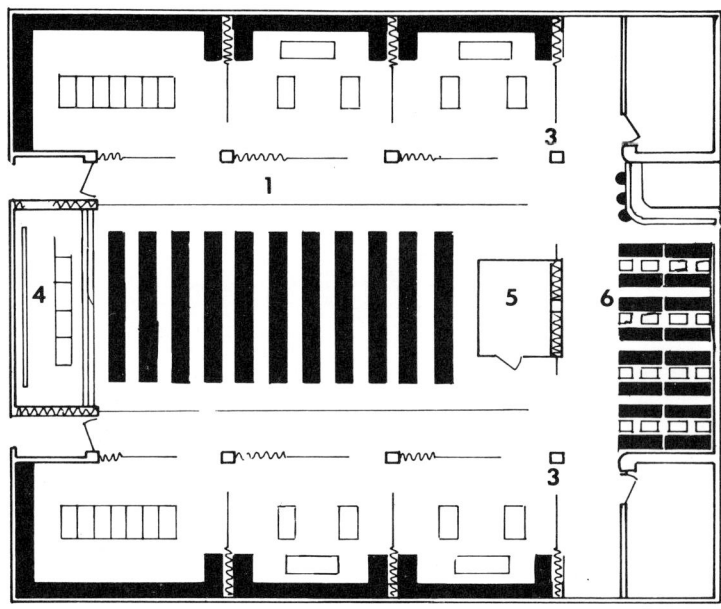

1. MULTI-PURPOSE CONFERENCE CENTRE	Our conference premises include a multi-purpose centre with seating for 377. Additional rooms can be reserved also. If necessary the multi-purpose centre can be divided by soundproof folding partitions. Space at the sides is equipped with large glass screens for various types of exhibition.
2. MAIN CONFERENCE AUDITORIUM	The centre of the multi-purpose hall is the main conference auditorium seating 124. If desired this can be used as a cinema.
3. AUXILIARY ROOMS	On either side of the main conference hall is seating space for 110. This space can be divided by folding partitions into 6 smaller rooms, the smallest of which seats 26.
4. CHAIRMAN'S PLATFORM	On the chairman's platform there is a panel discussion table for 5 speakers. Behind it is a projection screen.
5. FILM PROJECTION ROOM	There are 3 film projectors in all, two of them 35mm and one 16 mm. There are 2 slide projectors—one of them with sound synchronization. The sound reproduction is

through 4-channel stereo equipment with special amplifiers.

BAR The multi-purpose conference centre has a bar seating 33.

CONFERENCE EQUIPMENT

Every seat in the main conference auditorium has a writing table and an intercommunication device with amplifier and microphone for use during debates.

The rooms at the sides have their own conference equipment which can be used either together with that in the main auditorium or separately.

The conference centre is equipped with a videotape recorder, camera and 7 monitor TV sets for videotaping presentations and viewing them again. Speakers' own videotapes can also be shown.

The film projection room has both film and slide projectors.

Both 8 and 16 mm colour films and slides can be viewed through the TV monitor sets. All normal conference equipment is available, including overhead projectors for transparencies, a photocopier, flip charts, typewriters, etc.

Movable equipment
2   8mm film projectors   3 projection screens
8 overhead projectors   2 tape recorders
1 epidiascope   9 flip-charts
2 cassette recorders   6 slide projectors

Fix equipment
2   35 mm film projectors
2   16 mm film projectors
1 transistorized amplifier
equipment for simultaneous interpreting

Hotel English

Project work

With the aid of the advertisement "Are you planning . . ." and the layout plan of the conference facilities on board plus the list of equipment, try to arrange an answer to the following problems:

1. A Dutch firm Discogram, Rotterdam, wish to arrange their Annual Conference. A new series of popular records for the season ahead is to be presented. They are, therefore, extremely interested in the nature of your technical equipment.
   They will have a total of 120 sales representatives from all over Europe and there will be three official languages. They are arranging to bring along a leading pop band to entertain the conference during their off-duty hours.
   Don't forget to mention the other facilities on board, including nightclub, discos, roulette and bar facilities and the saunas.

2. JHK, a leading Japanese manufacturer of tractors, would like to hold a retail conference on ship. You will have to organize the whole thing. It might be a nice gesture to arrange for every member of the party to receive a complimentary gift. There will be in excess of 150 delegates.

3. Uhem, Germany, want to arrange a Sales Meeting cum Seminar for 46 sales representatives to discuss their new communication system. They will be extremely interested in high-quality, reliable and up-to-date technical equipment. Try to arrange something to satisfy them.

Useful phrases

I can give you some information on the prices.

Our new Japanese video equipment costs $45 for three hours.

The overhead projector is 35 Fmk a day.

I'm glad to be of assistance.

We could test out the microphones.

The acoustics are very good.

It accommodates about 500 people.

Chapter 10
CAN I SEE THE MANAGER?

Politely dealing with complaints

All members of a hotel staff must be ready to deal with complaints—some of them genuine, some silly—politely but firmly. Here are some examples:

1 *a.* Is that the Manager?
 b. Speaking. Can I be of any assistance?
 a. Could you speed up your switchboard a bit please? I booked a call to Brussels a good twenty minutes ago and I haven't had a reply yet.
 b. Well, perhaps they are rather busy at this time of the day. After all, we are an hour ahead of Belgium.
 a. I know that, but I could have dialled myself direct in no time at all.
 b. We do like to route the calls through the operator and then there can be no misunderstanding about the charges, I'm sure you understand.
 a. No, I suppose it would be difficult to check the cost of directly-dialled calls, but nevertheless I do have to put through an important call to Brussels.
 b. I'll get on to them myself and see what the delay is, then call you back as soon as I know anything.

Hotel English

2 *a.* And what seems to be the trouble sir?
  b. They don't want to let me into the nightclub.
  a. Well, I'm afraid there is an entrance charge sir.
  b. But damn it all—I am a resident. It's ridiculous.
  a. I'm very sorry sir, but you see it is something of a special evening. Our guest star this evening is Sammy Davis Junior and I'm afraid that the tickets do cost 250 marks each. I could see if there are any left if you would like one. We generally try to keep a few back for the residents.
  b. Good Lord. That's nearly £35. No, on second thoughts, I don't think I'll bother. Could you have them send up a bottle of scotch to my room. I'll entertain myself instead.
  a. Very good sir. That is room 634, isn't it?

3 *a.* Good evening sir. I'm the Assistant Manager.
  b. How nice.
  a. Yes, I'm afraid we've had a complaint about the noise from your neighbour across the corridor. He's trying to get some sleep as he has an early start tomorrow. I'm sure you understand.
  b. Oh, I see.
  a. Do you think it might be possible to ask your friends to be a little quieter? We do like to give our guests a chance of getting a good night's sleep. It is well after 11.
  b. Oh, I'm so sorry. I do apologize. I suppose we were talking rather loudly. It's just that we've signed a very important contract. We were having a bit of a celebration.
  a. I'm pleased to hear it. Shall I ask Room Service to bring you some coffee?
  b. No, that won't be necessary. We were just about to pack up anyway.
  a. Thank you sir and good night to you.

4 *a.* Could I see the Manager please? I have a complaint.
  b. Can I help you madam?
  a. Yes. Did you have this room checked before we moved in? There's not a scrap of lavatory paper and the toilet doesn't flush properly, the water doesn't run away in the

Can I See the Manager?

shower and I would like an extra pillow. What have you to say to that?

b. I'm extremely sorry to hear that. I'll attend to it right away. The housekeeper usually checks every room before new guests move in. We have been extremely busy with a large conference.

a. That's no way to run a hotel. One doesn't expect this sort of thing in a well-run hotel.

b. No madam. I do apologize. It's unusual. We do try to check the rooms as thoroughly as possible. Just the one pillow was it? Is there anything else?

a. Well, your thermostatically-controlled air-conditioning doesn't seem to be working too well. It's as hot as hell up there.

b. I'll just adjust the regulator for you and I think you'll find it a little cooler in a short time. I'll also send someone along right away to look at the toilet and shower.

---

5 *a.* What in heaven's name happened to my baggage?

b. Are you with Mr Grey's party?

a. Yeah, and my suitcases have disappeared. What are you going to do about it?

b. You did put your cases outside the door by 8, did you sir?

a. Yeah. Well, maybe it was a bit later, say about 9.30. We didn't get to bed till well after 3 a.m.

b. I see. Well, the bellboys would have picked up the group's luggage just after eight and brought it down to the main entrance. You do remember putting the cases outside the door?

a. Yeah, sure we did. Do you think we're nuts or something?

b. I'll just check with the bellboy and see if he remembers collecting any baggage from outside room 369.

a. Yeah. Two soft pig-skin suitcases with blue and white stickers on them. One of them had my movie equipment in it.

b. The bellboy says there was nothing outside 369 except a pair of brown shoes which he had cleaned and returned about 9.20.

Hotel English

a. Yeah. I put the cases out when I took my shoes in.

b. Oh, I see. In that case it looks as if they might have been stolen. I'm afraid this will have to be reported to the police. I'm extremely sorry that this has happened, but you realize that we cannot keep tabs on everyone in the hotel. I'll deal with this personally and see what can be done. Perhaps you would be good enough to give a list of the contents and a complete description. It is rare for things to disappear but it does happen sometimes.

Practice

Exercise I   Use the following cue-words, which summarize the five conversations above, to reproduce the dialogues as far as possible in your own words.

1. Booked call to Brussels 20 mins. ago. Still haven't been connected.
   Busy. Time difference.
   Could have dialled direct.
   Need to go through operator to get correct charges.
   Urgent.
   Check with switchboard.

2. Refused admission to nightclub.
   Entrance charge.
   Resident.
   Special show. 250 marks for ticket. See if there's any left.
   Too expensive. Bottle of scotch in room instead.

3. Complaint from neighbour about noise in room.
   Sorry.
   Reduce noise.
   Reasons for noise. Apology.

4. Room not checked. No paper. Toilet doesn't work. Shower blocked.
   Most unusual. Sorry. Very busy.
   Not good enough.
   Check room. Attend to problems immediately. Anything else?
   Air conditioning not right.
   Will get it adjusted.

5   Suitcases gone.
    Put out by 8?
    Perhaps a bit later.
    Bellboys would have collected all luggage by 8.
    2 pig-skin cases.
    Took shoes in when cases put out.
    Must have been stolen. Report to police. Apology. List of contents needed.

Exercise II   Look at the Useful phrases on page 102 to help you take the part of the Manager in dealing with the complaints that follow.

1   I didn't get my breakfast in my room this morning though I ordered it last night.
2   The towels in my room have not been changed.
3   My neighbours are very noisy. Could you tell them to be quite?
4   There is a mistake in my bill.
5   My shower doesn't work.
6   I booked a double room with shower and you have given me a single room.
7   There is a large spider in my bath.
8   I want a complete refund.

Exercise III   What would you say to the person in question when dealing with the following situations?

1   A person arrives at the nightclub wearing only a tee-shirt and jeans.
2   A famous pop star is disturbing other guests by having a noisy party in his room.
3   A guest insists on taking a lady friend, who is not registered at the hotel, into his room.
4   A businessman from the Far East wants his bill sent to his firm in Indonesia for settlement.
5   A guest is complaining about the slow service behind the bar.

Hotel English

Useful phrases

Can I help you sir?
Can I be of any assistance madam?
Excuse me, but could you tell me what the trouble is?
We'll attend to it right away.
I'll call you back as soon as I can.
We had a complaint about the noise.
There seems to be some misunderstanding.
I'm afraid that is not possible madam.
That's rather difficult I'm afraid sir.

Chapter 11
CHECKING OUT

At the Cashier's Office

Cashier   Good morning sir. Can I help you?
James   I'd like to settle my bill.
Cashier   Certainly sir. It's Mr Arkwright isn't it?
James   That's right. I'm leaving today, so I'd like to have my bill.
Cashier   Just a moment sir . . . Here we are. Four nights at 93 marks, and here are the meals that you had at the hotel. That makes a total of 665 marks.
James   Um—what's this amount here?
Cashier   That's the twelve and a half per cent service charge.
James   Ah, so service is included. Don't you go in for tipping then in Finland?
Cashier   Not very much sir.
James   Right. Now, can I pay by Eurocard?
Cashier   Certainly sir. May I have the card please?
James   Here you are.
Cashier   Would you sign here please?

Cashier   Good morning madam.
Lady   I'd like to change a traveller's cheque.
Cashier   Yes madam. And for how much?
Lady   Twenty-five pounds.

Hotel English

Cashier Would you sign here please?
Lady What rate are you giving?
Cashier Seven point nine Finnmarks to the pound.
Lady I see, so that'll be—um—er—.
Cashier That makes 197 marks 50 pennies madam. Here you are.
Lady Thank you. But could I have some more change?
Cashier Shall I split this 50 mark note into fives and tens?
Lady Let me see—ten is a bit more than a pound, and five—. Yes, that will be all right.
Cashier Thank you madam.

Practice

You are the cashier at a hotel in England. Some guests want to change foreign currency and ask for the rates of exchange. Refer to the rates given and answer the questions.

RATES OF EXCHANGE (UK sterling)

Austria SCH	34.30	Netherlands G	5.21
Belgium FR	77.25	Norway KR	12.53
Canada $	2.86	Portugal ESC	129.53
Denmark KR	14.72	Spain PTA	189.00
France FR	11.07	Sweden KR	10.74
Greece DR	131.00	Switzerland FR	4.37
Italy LIT	2255	USA $	2.387
Japan YN	512.00	Yugoslavia DR	79.50

1 I'd like to change 100 Swedish crowns. What rate are you giving?
2 Can I pay in dollars? What's the rate today?
3 How much would I get for 2000 French francs?
4 I'd like to change some German marks. What's the rate of exchange?
5 What would you give me for my Italian lira please?

Checking Out

Paying the bill

Here is the conversation in which the Receptionist explains Mr Colyer's bill:

Guest	Could I have my bill please?
Receptionist	Certainly sir. What name is it?
Guest	Colyer, Robert Colyer from room 222.
Receptionist	Here we are sir. That comes to 258 marks and 76 pennies altogether.
Guest	But I've only been here one night. Do you think you could go through it item by item and explain it all?
Receptionist	That first number is your room number 222.
Guest	Oh I see. I thought it might have been the charge for my telex to Athens, but that does seem a bit cheap all the way to Greece.
Receptionist	No, that is the third item—20 marks for your telex. The second entry here is the restaurant—main lunch yesterday—a total of 53 marks. Item six is 15 marks for the garage.
Guest	I had dinner in the steak house, is that this 107 marks here?
Receptionist	No sir. The steak house was 34 marks 76 pennies. Item 9 is a mistake.
Guest	Thank goodness for that. I was beginning to think that Finland really is an expensive country.
Receptionist	Item 10 is the 140 marks for your room and item 13 is the mistake corrected.
Guest	Oh, that's not so bad. Did you remember that I had breakfast?
Receptionist	Yes sir. That appears here. Item 17, 12 marks and I believe you also bought some newspapers, that's the 4 marks here making a grand total of 258 marks and 76 pennies. I'll just check it again for you. yes, I'm afraid I can't make it any less for you.
Guest	Not at all. You've been most helpful. I just wanted to make sure that's all.
Receptionist	Only too pleased to be of assistance. And we hope to see you again some day.
Guest	Thank you and goodbye.

Hotel English

NAME	ROBERT COLYER		
HOME TOWN	EDINBURGH		**BILL**
ROOM NUMBER	222	NO. OF PERSONS	1
PRICE	140,-	DATE	26.6.

#					
1		78 555=26	N°	0002.22 : :	ROOM NUMBER
2		2	A	0033.00 : RAV	RESTAURANT STEAK HOUSE
3		3	A 7	0020.00 : PUH	TELEPHONE
4		74 555=26	US	0053.00 : :	
5		5	B	0053.00 DEB :	
6		6	B	0015.00 : HOT PALV	GARAGE
7		7	B 9	0034.76 : RAV	RESTAURANT MAIN LUNCH
8		78 559=26	US	0102.76 : :	
9		9	B	0107.26 DEB :	A MISTAKE
10		10	B	0140.00 : HUON	ROOM RATE
11		78 562=26	US	0247.26 : :	
12		12	B	0247.26 DEB :	
13		13	B	0107.26 KRED :	MISTAKE CORRECTED
14		14	B	0102.76 DEB :	
15		78 565=26	US	0242.76 : :	
16		16	A	0242.76 DEB :	CORRECTED TOTAL
17		17	A 5	0012.00 : RAV	BREAKFAST
18		18	A	0004.00 : PORT	RECEPTION PAPERS
19	№ 004774	78 568=27	US	0258.76 : :	TOTAL
20		20			
21		21			

Checking Out

Practice

Using Mr. Colyer's bill as an example, explain this bill for Mr. Legros

NAME	Mr Bernard LEGROS		**BILL**
HOME TOWN	Paris, France		
ROOM	356	NO. OF PERSONS	1
PRICE	135:—	DATE	3.4.-78

#			
1	78 989≥-3	N° 0003.56	: :
2	2	B 0012.40	: PUH
3	3	B2 0020.00	: HOT PALV
4	78 989≥-3	US 0032.40	: :
5	5	B 0034.20 DEB	:
6	6	B 0135.00	: HUON
7	78 990≥-3	US 0169.20	: :
8	8	B 0169.20 DEB	:
9	9	B 0034.20 KRED	:
10	10	B 0032.40 DEB	:
11	78 991≥-3	US 0167.40	: :
12	12	B 0167.40 DEB	:
13	13	B 0012.40 KORJ	:
14	14	B 0012.40	: RAV
15	78 992≥-3	US 0167.40	: :
16	16	A 0167.40 DEB	:
17	17	A 0015.00	: RAV
18	78 994≥-4	US 0182.40	: :
19	N° 004841 19		
20	20		
21	21		

Hotel English

Useful phrases

Would you please settle your bill at the Cashier's desk?
That makes a total of (700) marks
    will be (700) marks in all
Service is included
We accept cheques with a banker's card
How are you paying?
I'll just take down the particulars if I may
Don't forget to leave your key at Reception
Do you have a credit card?
Item (4) refers to (your telephone calls)
To pay in cash
    by travellers cheque
    in foreign currency
    by voucher
    by signing the bill
    by credit card
    by cheque

Chapter 12
POLITE PHRASES

(A selection of the phrases in this unit is recorded on the cassette)

Greeting

Meeting friends

How are you?
How's life with you?
How're things?
How's it going then?

Replies
Fine thanks, and you?
Oh, not too bad, and you?
Can't complain, and you?
All right thanks, and you?

If you haven't seen the person for a long time, you can say:
Haven't seen you for ages!
or Fancy meeting you!

Introducing people
This is (Mr Jackson)—This is (Miss Wilson)
May I introduce you to (Mr Jackson)?
I'd like you to meet (Mr Jackson)

The people who are introduced say to each other:
How d'you do?
Pleased to meet you (Mr Jackson)

The next time you meet, if you don't know the person very well, you can say:
Good morning (until 12 noon)
Good afternoon (until about 5pm)   The reply is the same
Good evening (after about 5pm)

Hotel English

Greeting guests in a hotel
Good (afternoon) (Mr Jackson). Welcome to the (Hotel Neptune)
I trust you had a good journey.
I hope you'll enjoy your stay here
I hope your stay will be a pleasant one
If there's anything you need, just ring Reception

Conversation

Christine   Look, George. There's somebody waving. I think he's waving to you.

George   Good gracious, that's Michael Jones. I haven't seen him for years. We were in Greece together.

Christine   Well, he's coming over.

George   Hello Michael. How are you?

Michael   Fine thanks. I haven't seen you for ages.

George   I'd like you to meet my girlfriend Christine. Christine, this is Michael Jones.

Mary   How do you do? George has often talked about being in Greece with you.

Michael   How do you do, Christine. I'm very pleased to meet you.

George   Are you in a hurry, Michael?

Michael   Not really, why?

George   Let's go and have a drink somewhere and catch up on old times.

Polite Phrases

Leaving

If you don't know the person very well, you can say:
Goodbye. It was so nice meeting you.

If you know the person well, you can say:
Cheerio/Bye bye/Bye/See you

If it's late, you can say:
Goodnight

General phrases for departure
Well, I really must be off now/on my way
If you'll excuse me I really ought to be going (formal)
Look at the time! I must dash (informal)
Well, all the best
See you later (for a meeting later the same day)

Conversation

Michael   Well, it's been lovely seeing you but I really must be off.
George   Yes, we must be on our way too. It was nice seeing you again.
Michael   It was nice meeting you, Christine.
Mary   I enjoyed meeting you too. Goodbye Michael.
Michael   Goodbye. Cheerio George

Practice

What would you say if:

you met an old friend called John?

you wanted to introduce Mr. Matthews to your friend Tony Wilson?

you had to leave a group of friends?

you had just been introduced to Miss Johnson?

you were going to meet your friend later on in the evening?

you had to leave someone you had just been introduced to?

Hotel English

Please and thank you

'Please' is seldom used on its own. It is normally used in a phrase when you want something. Notice that English people use 'please' and 'thank you' quite a lot.

    Would you mind (opening the window) please?—Not at all.
    Would you (pass the salt) please?—Of course.
    Could you (hand me that book please)?—Here you are.

'Please' is not used alone when you give something:

    Would you like some coffee?
    Here's your coffee.

Formal thanks
Thank you for (inviting me)
Thank you for (a lovely weekend)   *Replies*
Thank you for (your help)
It was so kind of you (to help out)

    Not at all
    You're welcome
    It's a pleasure
    Don't mention it

Less formal thanks
Thanks ever so much
Thanks a lot

Reply to both:
That's all right

If you are offered something, you say:
Yes please (if you want it)
or No thank you (if you don't want it)

Practice

What would you say if:

you wanted someone to close the door?
someone asked you to pass him the ashtray?
someone invited you for a drink?
someone thanked you for a gift you gave them?
you handed someone his coat?

Polite Phrases

Apologizing

If you don't hear or understand what the other person says you can say:
  Pardon? I beg your pardon? I'm sorry? What did you say?

If you have made a mistake or done something that you didn't mean to you say:
  Sorry./I'm so sorry./I'm very sorry./I'm terribly sorry./I do apologize

The answer to that might be:
  That's all right./Not at all./Never mind./No harm done

If you have to interrupt someone for something you can say:
  I'm sorry to disturb/bother you. — That's all right.
                                     Please go ahead
                                     Not at all.

Excuse me. - Yes?
May I interrupt you for a moment?—Of course.
  I'm afraid I'll have to interrupt you.—That's all right.

Formal apologies
  I'm so sorry (I'm late)
  I do apologize for (being late)
  Please forgive me (for being late)

Practice

What would you say if:

you arrived late for a formal meeting?
you trod on someone's toes?
you had to wake someone up late at night?
you had to interrupt a conversation?
someone apologized for pushing into you?
someone apologized for disturbing you?

Hotel English

Other useful phrases

Formal regards:
   Give my regards to (your family)—Thank you I will.
   Give my best regards to (Janet)—Thank you I will.

Less formal:
   Give my love to (Mary)—Thanks, I will.
   Remember me to (your parents)—Of course, and me to (yours)

When someone is ill:
   I hope you get better soon.
   I hope you soon get well again.

When someone has a birthday:
   Happy Birthday/Many Happy Returns—Thank you.

When someone is going somewhere:
   Have a good time—Thanks.
   Have a good trip—Thanks, I'm sure I shall.
   Have a nice weekend—Thanks, the same to you.

Something good has happened:
   Congratulations—Thanks.

Asking for permission:
   Do you mind if I smoke?
   May I be excused for a moment?

Practice

What would you say if:
   your friend was going on holiday?
   your friend was getting married?
   you wished to smoke?
   someone was going off to a party?
   you wanted your friend to pass on your good wishes to her husband?

English as a Second Language

Helen Brennan Memorial Library